For Kathleen McCartney
with much appreciation
and admiration

[illegible]

IN THE COUNTRY OF EMPTY CROSSES

IN THE COUNTRY OF EMPTY CROSSES

The Story of a Hispano Protestant Family in Catholic New Mexico

---

ARTURO MADRID · *Photographs by Miguel Gandert*

Trinity University Press, San Antonio

Trinity University Press gratefully acknowledges the support of the following in the publication of this book

Ron and Genie Calgaard

Maureen and Robert Decherd

Sarah E. Harte and John S. Gutzler Fund of the San Antonio Area Foundation

Terry Saario and Lee Lynch

For Amalia Devereux, Nicolás Alistiano, and Gabriela Aranza; Arturo Carlos, Raúl Lorca, and Marisa Rafaela Madrid, *para que sepan*; and in memory of my heretic and interloper ancestors, *que en paz descansen*

††† CONTENTS

PREFACE

† † † Throughout my career many a friend asked when I was going to write my memoirs. Never, I thought. I did not consider myself a worthy subject for a memoir that expounded on my experiences and accomplishments, real or imagined. And my *protestante* upbringing did not permit any expression that might be considered boasting. Plus, a memoir that explored the dark side of my psyche or unearthed familial secrets held no attraction for me. *Protestantes* are anticonfessional by nature. We keep our skeletons buried, and deeply so. Nor was I caught up, as so many of my fellow Hispanos are, in establishing a genealogy that confirmed our European origins and denied our indigenous roots.

But my familial history and its trajectory did arouse my curiosity. The Hispano population of New Mexico does not fit the usual imagining of Mexicans in this society, and my family less so. We are not immigrants, nor Catholic, nor poor or uneducated or illiterate or monolingual. My forebearers colonized New Mexico in the seventeenth century. An ancestor, Roque Madrid, wrote a journal about his campaign against the Apache Navajos in 1703. Both my paternal and maternal great-grandfathers were literate, owned and read the Bible, and became *protestantes*. My paternal grandfather completed theological studies at a Presbyterian school for evangelists in 1894. My parents, as well as multiple uncles, aunts, and cousins, were college-educated, bilingual, and profoundly bicultural professionals. And my family was not unique in that regard. Ours was an experience shared by the *protestante* community of New Mexico.

This book is neither autobiography nor family history, but rather a retracing, a recollection, and a remembrance. In the last decade and a half I have visited and revisited the spaces and places my ancestors occupied, and traced and retraced their routes and paths. The experience is rendered in Spanish as *recorrer* or *hacer un recorrido*, meaning to travel through, to traverse. Some of my *recorridos* took me through familiar spaces, but many were new and unknown to me. In the process I visited family and friends to gather—*recolectar*—their stories and asked them to recall—*recordar*—the doings and the existence of the extended *protestante* community of New Mexico. For many years I have been summoning up, putting together, and giving coherence to that dismembered body of experience—or *re-membering* it.

In the Country of Empty Crosses owes its existence to my beloved *compañera*, Antonia I. Castañeda. The work was initially propelled by the metaphorical push she gave me shortly after I joined the Trinity University faculty in 1993. "What," she asked me, "are you going to work on at this stage in your life?" The second was a figurative shove. In the summer of 1995, undoubtedly weary of my complaints about the Texas heat and the refrigerated air that alleviated it, Antonia said, "Go explore your *protestante* heritage." The resulting project has nurtured me for the past fifteen years.

I had good companions in my *recorridos*. My father, the late Arturo Teófilo; my spouse, Antonia; my sister, Concha Del Mar; my son, Raúl Lorca; my childhood friend, Alfonso de Herrera; and three *compañeros* of my mature years, Estevan Rael-Gálvez and Juan Ríos, who are vitally present in my narrative, and Miguel Gandert, whose photographs give visual texture to my words.

My explorations were facilitated and enriched by multiple friends, all more knowledgeable about New Mexico than I. They explained its complex history, corrected my misperceptions, identified sources, and encouraged my explorations. I make special note of Miguel Gandert, Deena González, Phillip Gonzales, William Gonzales, Ramón Gutiérrez, Enrique Lamadrid, E. A. Mares, Gabriel Meléndez, Richard Nostrand, Michael A. Olivas, the late Alfonso Ortiz, Estevan Rael-Gálvez, Al Regensberger, Sylvia Rodríguez, Roberto Torres, Carlos Trujillo, and Chris Wilson.

Many are the persons who gave me guidance and direction; accompanied me; related their stories to me; provided me with encouragement, inspiration, and understanding; and extended support, shelter, and sustenance.

My journey of discovery took me first to the southeastern edge of the llano, a region my paternal ancestors settled in the first half of the nineteenth century, to visit my friend John Bassett. I wrote about that and subsequent odysseys in the comfort of John and Nolana Bassett's Santa Fe home, located within walking distance of the seventeenth- and eighteenth-century residences of my Madrid and Barela ancestors.

The main narrative, however, first took form at Las Palomas, the San Isidro de Tesuque home of two extraordinary individuals, Terry Saario and Leland Lynch, longtime and loving friends whose interest in the project sustained it over the years. Together with my late father, they constituted my first audience and have remained my most enthusiastic and supportive one. Much of the subsequent narrative was produced in the beauty, comfort, and quiet of Las Palomas.

Charles and Beth Miller, along with Terry and Lee, are truly the book's *madrinas* and *padrinos*. Charles and Beth gave me a second home and a writing studio at Sol y Sombra in Santa Fe for many years. Their friendship and generosity permitted me to reflect, reconsider, and rewrite, activities essential to a memoir.

Tía Leonardita Barela and cousins Fidencia and Susie fed me and put me up during my many visits to Las Truchas, as did my uncle and aunt, Ray and Ruth Barela, during my extended stays in Albuquerque. Mornings and evenings I sat at the kitchen table with Tía, Susie, and Fide or with Ray and Ruth taking notes as they recalled names, dates, and places and wove and interwove their multiple and frequently contradictory stories. My aunt Viola Barela Martínez and cousins Aurora Tafoya González and Lorraine Romero Aguilar provided names, dates, and documents and revealed family histories otherwise kept hidden.

In the summer of 2001, Pat and Rudolfo Anaya generously extended to me their home in Jémez Springs, where I wrote about growing up in La Tierra Amarilla.

I count among my literary models and advisers several remarkable artists: Sandra Cisneros, Alicia Gaspar de Alba, Rolando Hinojosa-Smith, Pat Mora, Kristen Naca, Emma Pérez, John Phillip Santos, and Carmen Tafolla. They taught me to distill my experiences and to limn my words.

It was my good fortune to be among the early Macondistas, the participants in the Macondo Writers' Workshop established by Sandra Cisneros. I was the scholar, the critic, the elder statesman to whom my fellow writers deferred, but they read and critiqued my stories, pushed me to expand them, and urged me to search for more. All published their creations long before I did. Their example spurred me on. They know who they are, and I thank them for their investment in me.

A writer yearns for readers. An aspirant one is grateful for listeners. Over the years multiple audiences have heard my stories. Some listeners, I hope, will revisit them here. I first told the story of Papá Albino, my paternal great-grandfather, in 1997 when I delivered the Mangels Lecture at the University of Washington at the invitation of Lauro Flores. "Herejes" had its first formal reading in 1999 at the Trinity University faculty research seminar. In fall 1999 my *comadre*, Marysa Navarro, invited me to Dartmouth College, where I read "The Chosen People." Teresa Márquez sponsored a reading of "The Interloper" at the University of New Mexico's Zimmerman Library in 2000. Roberto Torres, then New Mexico State Historian, hosted a reading of "La Tierra Amarilla" in 2001 under the auspices of the New Mexico Genealogical Society. Nicolás Kanellos invited me to read "Santa Trinidad" at the second annual Recovering the Hispanic Religious Heritage Conference in 2003. "Canicas" debuted at the National Hispanic Cultural Center in 2004, at the invitation of Carlos Vásquez, director of its History and Literary Arts Program. I thank one and all for hosting me and thus helping me realize this book.

My appointment as the Norene R. and T. Frank Murchison Distinguished Professor at Trinity University, brought about by my friend Ronald K. Calgaard in his capacity as Trinity University's president, provided me with the opportunity to explore the historical experience of the Hispano Protestants. Ron's support of my undertakings in the past twenty-five years, including service on the board of directors of the Tomás Rivera Center during my tenure as its president, has been unqualified and unremitting.

Shortly after I arrived in San Antonio, Robert Decherd, who served as a trustee of the Tomás Rivera Center, invited me to join the board of directors of the Belo Corporation, of which he was CEO. That appointment allowed me to dedicate myself to the memoir instead of having to seek summer employment. Maureen and Robert Decherd have been steadfast friends and supporters over the years.

I have received considerable financial support from Trinity University for my research. In addition to having a generous research allowance, I have benefited from two sabbaticals during my tenure. The University of New Mexico Center for Regional Studies and its director, Tobias Durán, provided me with a fellowship and an office in the Chicano Studies Program in the summer of 1999.

My quest led me first to the Menaul Historical Library in Albuquerque, then to the New Mexico State Archives in Santa Fe, and then to the Presbyterian Historical Society in Philadelphia, and I hereby acknowledge and express my appreciation for the access provided to me.

Barbara Ras, director of Trinity University Press, pushed me to submit the manuscript to her and assigned it to a thoughtful and sympathetic reader, Gregory McNamee, who reviewed it, edited it, and declared it worthy of publication, thus bringing to a close an odyssey of a decade and a half. *In the Country of Empty Crosses* is graced by the remarkable photographs of Miguel Gandert. The final product is a testament to the exceptional editing skills of Sarah Nawrocki, managing editor of Trinity University Press, and to the magnificent artistry of designer Kristina Kachele. *Les quedo sumamente agradecido.*

IN THE COUNTRY OF EMPTY CROSSES

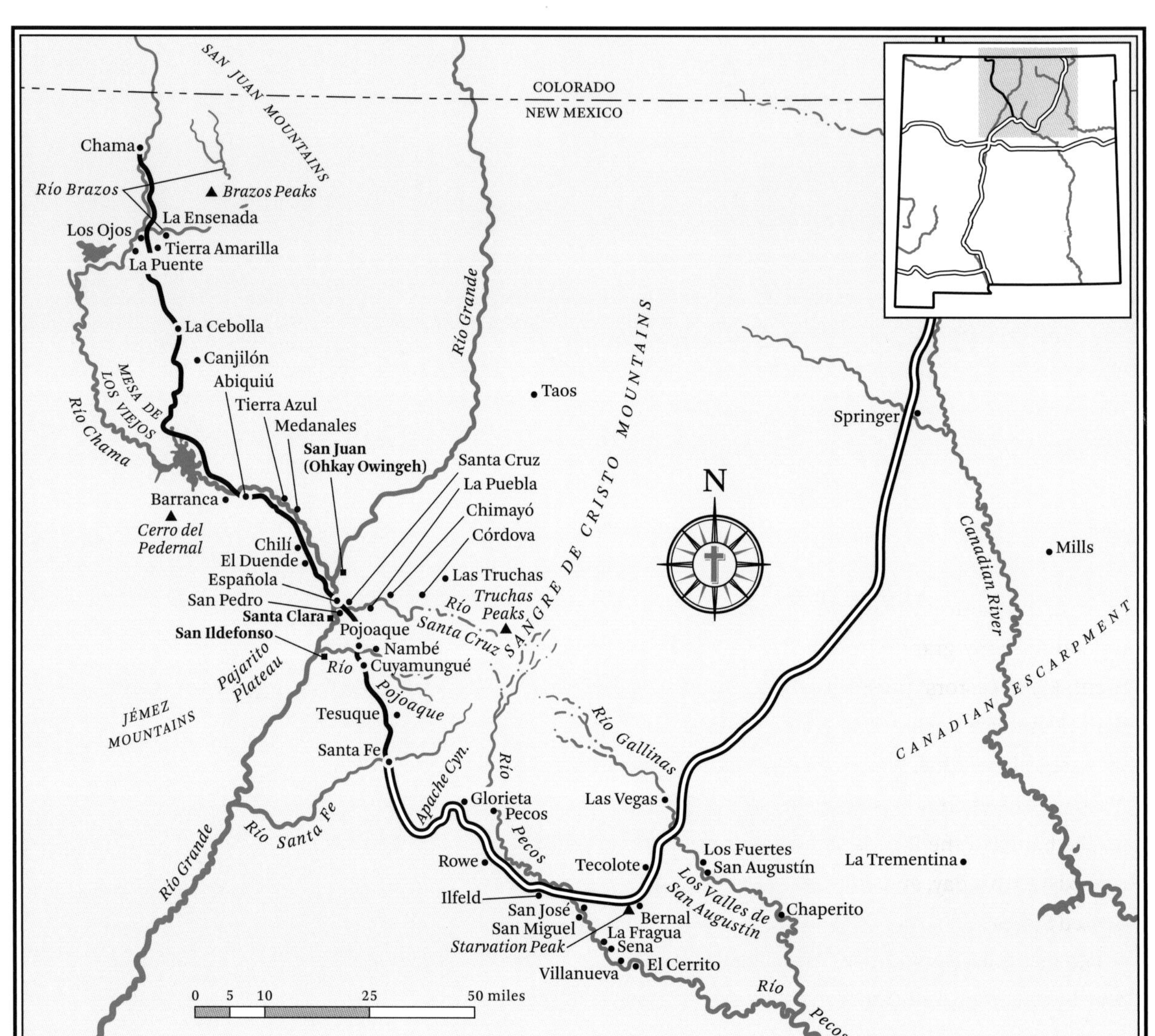
COLORADO
NEW MEXICO
SAN JUAN MOUNTAINS
Chama
Río Brazos
Brazos Peaks
La Ensenada
Los Ojos
Tierra Amarilla
La Puente
La Cebolla
Canjilón
Abiquiú
Tierra Azul
Medanales
MESA DE LOS VIEJOS
Río Chama
San Juan
(Ohkay Owingeh)
Barranca
Cerro del Pedernal
Chilí
El Duende
Española
San Pedro
Santa Clara
San Ildefonso
Pojoaque
Nambé
Cuyamungué
Santa Cruz
La Puebla
Chimayó
Córdova
Las Truchas
Truchas Peaks
Río Santa Cruz
Río Grande
Taos
SANGRE DE CRISTO MOUNTAINS
N
Río Pojoaque
Pajarito Plateau
JÉMEZ MOUNTAINS
Tesuque
Santa Fe
Apache Cyn.
Río Santa Fe
Río Grande
Glorieta
Pecos
Río Pecos
Rowe
Ilfeld
San José
San Miguel
Starvation Peak
Río Gallinas
Las Vegas
Tecolote
Bernal
La Fragua
Sena
El Cerrito
Villanueva
Los Fuertes
San Augustín
Los Valles de San Augustín
Chaperito
La Trementina
Río Pecos
Springer
Canadian River
Mills
CANADIAN ESCARPMENT
0 5 10 25 50 miles

AND WHERE ARE YOU FROM?

† † † My name is Arturo Madrid. I am a citizen of the United States, as were my parents, my grandparents, and their parents and grandparents before them. My ancestors' presence in what is now part of the United States antedates Plymouth Rock. I am the descendant of the Spanish-Mexican colonists who settled the upper Rio Grande watershed of New Mexico, known as the Rio Arriba, at the end of the sixteenth century. The communities they established on the banks of the Rio Grande and its tributaries over the next three centuries exist to this day, and they are among the oldest colonial settlements in the United States.

I do not, however, fit those mental sets that define America and Americans. My physical appearance, my speech patterns, my name, my profession create a text that confuses its reader. I possess the coloring and other physical manifestations of my mestizo ancestors. My "accent" is neither the pronounced one of southerners or New Englanders nor the nondescript one of westerners or midwesterners, but rather one common to people of Mexican origin in this country. My normal experience is to be asked, "And where are you from?" The question presupposes that I am not from here, that we—the Indo-Hispano population of the United States—are not part of the imagined community of the United States.

In 1848, with the signing of the Treaty of Guadalupe Hidalgo, which put an end to the U.S. war against Mexico and reduced the latter to half its original size, my great-great-grandparents and their progeny, residents of the Provincia de Nuevo México of the recently established nation of Mexico, became U.S. citizens. They had no choice in the matter. Whatever opinions they had on the subject are something I can only speculate about. They left no diaries. I have often wondered how they felt about the event that changed the course of their history, what they thought of the world that formed around them as a consequence, what their experiences with that world might have been. All became part of the new society, witnessed its raw character as well as its refined aspects, experienced its ravages as well as its benefits.

My great-grandparents and their families were willing members of the new society. They joined its Protestant churches, became literate in its language, attended its schools, took on its values and ways, participated in its institutions, and sought its benefits and opportunities. And yet, despite their efforts to integrate themselves into Anglo-American society, they were always perceived as and treated as the "foreign other." Their historical community saw them as heretics; in their new community they were interlopers.

From the time I was an adolescent through young adulthood, I was subject to a dual false consciousness. One branch is endemic, to a greater or lesser extent, to most Hispanos, as we *nuevomexicanos* call ourselves. It is an imagining that gives Hispanos a European identity and European origins and removes us from the supposed liability of being Mexicans; it is driven by hegemonic ideologies that disdain Africans and Asians, peoples indigenous to the Americas, and especially any mixtures thereof.

The second is related to the first. It is the imagining of Hispanos who in the latter half of the nineteenth century broke with their historical religious traditions and embraced the ones brought to them by their Anglo-American colonizers. This imagining is exceptionalist in character, setting communities apart and harkening to conflicts that occurred far away and long ago; it is not unlike the religious imaginings of the Israelites, who imagined themselves as the chosen people.

The former constitutes a well-explored if not well-understood terrain. The latter is neither explored nor understood—something I discovered in my review of the literature on Protestant activity among Hispanos. We are absent, by and large, from those histories, which have to do with the missionaries who came, in the words of Stephen B. Kearney, commanding general of the U.S. Army of the West, "to better [our] condition." The social history of Hispano Protestants, with all its ironies, contradictions, and paradoxes, is yet to be written. It is a history of considerable controversy, nonetheless richly illustrative of the complexities Latinas and Latinos face as we continue to struggle for standing in this society.

Over the past several years I have been exploring the experience of the Hispano Protestants as they came in contact with Anglo-American society in the nineteenth and early twentieth centuries. I have wandered through the geographical space my ancestors occupied; visited the communities, inhabited and abandoned, where they lived and died; explored their cemeteries; and, wherever I found them, conversed with the living. What I learned moved me to tell their stories, and mine, and in the process to contribute to a larger story—the conflictive historical experience of Hispanos in the past century and a half.

Ours is an American story, no less than those told by descendants of the settlers of the original thirteen colonies, or of the African slaves they imported, or of the immigrants who have come to this land over the past several centuries. Our story is intertwined with that of the original Americans, the indigenous populations of the Western Hemisphere. It is a story of heretics, righteous persons who acted on their beliefs, and of interlopers, brave persons who refused to know their place.

CAMPOHEREJE

† † † A low flagstone wall marks the *camposanto*, the consecrated field set aside for burial of the Christian faithful. An arroyo has begun to cut into it, the product of erosive, swirling water. Most of the east wall and the entire south wall have collapsed into the dry wash. The grave markers, like the walls, are made of flagstone. Many have toppled over. Water has seeped into the layers of soft material and separated them. Some lie broken in several pieces. Others have sunk into the earth.

This isolated streamside village, founded in the first half of the nineteenth century under the auspices of a *merced*, a community land grant, is where my father says Albino Madrid, his grandfather, lived before he moved his family upstream to Las Vegas. The village is located in a deep canyon formed by the Gallinas River as it works its way down from the eastern slopes of the Sangre de Cristo Mountains to the Pecos River. Its residents knew the area as Los Valles de San Augustín, the Valleys of Saint Augustine.

There is no human presence in this seemingly deserted village on a mid-August day. I set out my notebooks, reading materials, and lunch on a blanket and sit down in the shade of some Chinese elms, where I have parked my car. It is a mode I have developed over time. I am bait. If anyone is about, curiosity will get the best of him or her. As I eat my lunch I review the information I have copied from the *Registro de familia* in the Madrid family Bible. The family register lists the children, with their birth dates, of Albino Madrid and his brothers Pablo and Antonio. Deaths and marriages of family members are also recorded.

I hear bells in the distance. From the rim of the canyon above the village a herd of goats descends, watched over by a dog that approaches me warily. I am interloping in his space. He is small and scruffy. I throw him the remains of my sandwich, which he scarfs down. When he determines that nothing else is forthcoming and that I do not pose a danger to him or his flock, he approaches and smells me, then circles my car, sniffing each wheel before lifting his leg to leave his mark. Otherwise there is no sign of life.

After the herd meanders away I explore the deteriorating camposanto. Most of the tombstones are illegible. I copy the inscriptions from the ones that are readable. Many more bore the name Madrid on the occasion of my first visit, almost a decade ago. I regret that I did not write them down. Soon these too may be recorded only in my notebook and my memory. I walk among the graves and try without success to match the names on the tombstones with the ones I have copied from the Madrid Bible. The heat and glare of the midday sun discourage my efforts, and I abandon them.

After a long nap I stroll through the village. The houses look uninhabited. Many are boarded up. The village chapel in the middle of the plaza, however, has recently been plastered. The wooden cross standing in front of it is freshly painted. Imprinted in the plaster that covers the chapel's base are the words "Capilla de San Augustine."

I walk to the bluff overlooking the river. A trickle of water is visible in the streambed. A few mangy cattle graze across the river, in the confines of an ancient stone enclosure surrounded by rusty, gnarled barbed wire strung on weathered juniper posts. I walk upstream along the bluff to a large apple tree on the east bank of the acequia. Ground squirrels, large and dark, feast on green, misshapen apples lying on the ground. A snake plops into the ditch as I approach and swims downstream.

Late in the afternoon, as I walk back, I hear an engine in the distance. It is moving slowly upstream toward me. When I return to my car a truck and attached trailer carrying a pair of horses are parked next to it. Two children, a boy and girl, are in the apple tree across the road. Three men sit in the cab of the truck. I approach gingerly. This is their space. I greet them with "*Buenas tardes*." They nod. Then I offer my customary explanation: I'm just looking around. My family was from here. It is a time-tested formula.

They gaze off into the distance, but I know they are sizing me up from the corner of their eyes. The youngsters descend from the tree. They walk around my car, look in the windows, then climb back on the truck. In time I get the customary response. The man on the passenger side, who is wearing a gimme cap, asks about my family: "*¿Cómo se llamaban?*" Madrid, I answer.

He tells me he doesn't know any Madrids who live in the area. "There's a watering hole up above the Gallinas River called El Aguaje de los Madriles, though," he says, motioning with his chin in the universally shared gesture of the Hispanos of New Mexico toward the mesa behind us. Early Anglo travelers to New Mexico all comment on that gesture in their reports, but none of the maps I have consulted shows a Madrid watering hole.

As he talks he removes his cap and scratches his head. "Have you spoken with Lorenzo Gonzales, who lives here year-round? He goes by El Güero," he says. I shake my head. I've met no one by that name.

I invite him and his companions into the shade and offer them some coffee. They decline. They are drinking beer. But they drive the truck and trailer into the shade, and the driver and the man sitting on the passenger side get out.

The third man remains in the vehicle. He is disabled and clearly intoxicated. His companions light his cigarette and put a can of beer in his right hand.

Gimme Cap is young and heavyset and has not shaved in several days. His T-shirt does not cover his hairy paunch, and his trousers droop. The black high-tops he is wearing are unlaced. There are no markings on his cap, or else the elements have erased them. The crown is sweat-stained, and the bill has absorbed the oils and soils of a thousand handlings.

"What is your name?" he wants to know. "Who is your family? Where did you grow up?" It is an interrogation I am familiar with. My spouse, a Tejana by birth, says my fellow Hispanos behave like dogs when they meet. We circle each other, figuratively smelling each other out.

The questions spill from the man like water diverted from an acequia. What kind of car is that? How much does one of them cost? Why does it have Texas plates? Where do you live? How long have you lived there? What do you do there? Are you on vacation? When will you return to Texas? I answer each question in turn, measuring out the information he requests.

When he finally stops it is to walk around my car to relieve himself and peer through the windows. On his return he swallows what is left of his beer and takes a long drag on his cigarette. As he exhales he says, "*Aquí no hay Madriles.*" No one by that name lives around here. "There used to be some in La Trementina," he adds. "Did you know Andrés Madrid, originally from La Trementina, who died recently, at age eighty-six, in Las Vegas?"

I shake my head. I have visited La Trementina recently. It is located east of Las Vegas, at the foot of the Canadian Escarpment, which divides the high prairie, *las vegas*, from the lowland plains, *el llano*. La Trementina was one of the mission sites of the Presbyterian Church. It was populated by *herejes*—that is, heretics, as Hispano Catholics called their Protestant brethren. La Trementina is a ghost town. No one lives there.

The driver, who wears a black Stetson and dark glasses, has remained silent throughout the exchange. I estimate him to be in his mid-fifties, my age. He is slim and fit. The only bulge on him is created by the pack of Marlboro cigarettes in his shirt pocket. His western shirt is tailored, and his jeans are tightly creased. The cowboy boots he wears are hand-tooled and highly polished. There are no stains or marks on his hat. When he finally speaks, he tells me, "*Los Madriles no eran de aquí. Eran de Los Fuertes.*" His response catches me by surprise. Not from here? From a place called Los Fuertes? *Fuerte*, the Spanish word for fort, or a fortified area, resonates through me. A log structure in the Madrid family compound was called *el fuerte.* It stood next to Papá Albino's *fragua*, his blacksmith shop.

"*Los Gonzales, mi familia*," he continues, "were the founders of this plaza. The original name was Santa Gertrudis. It was located on a land grant over six thousand acres in size. The land grant is now less than six hundred acres, all in the valley. The forests and pastures on the mesas on either side of the valley passed into the hands of the Santa Fe Ring toward the end of the nineteenth century. These days the Japanese own most of those lands. They're fenced off." He pauses to draw on his cigarette.

"My great-great-great-grandfather Augustín was responsible for changing the name of the plaza to San Augustín," he tells me. "My great-great-grandfather, Miguel Albino, was killed by Apaches on the mesa above us while he was fetching some horses. My great-grandfather Marcos bought Los Fuertes and La Cañada from the Madrid family. The Madrids then moved out into the llano, to La Trementina. Along with the Bleas, the Jaramillos, the Luceros, and the Estradas."

"Where is Los Fuertes located?" I rush to ask. Before he can answer, my face flushed with excitement, I add, "Can one get into Los Fuertes, or is the place fenced off? Are there any ruins? Is there a camposanto?"

The Marlboro Man exhales cigarette smoke and takes a swallow of beer. "*Camposanto no*," he finally says. After a bit, he adds, "*Campohereje quizás*."

A burial ground for heretics, perhaps. I feel the blood drain from my face.

The wind has come up. A dust devil works its way toward us. We turn our heads and cover our eyes as it sweeps by. The man reaches down to wipe the dust off his boots. He clears his throat and spits. "*Era su religión*," he says. "*Protestantes*." They were Protestants.

He and his companions continue to pull at their beers and cigarettes. The children put their shoes on and climb into the truck. My coffee has gotten cold and bitter. Dust coats the rim of the cup. I toss the rest of the liquid and stow my thermos. We stand around in silence. I have no more questions for him.

In his own good time, the Marlboro Man tells me how to get to Los Fuertes. I listen but do not grasp his directions. Our measures do not match; our geometries do not coincide; our histories diverge. We take our leave quietly. I walk back up the slope and survey the camposanto, the long-abandoned Catholic burying field, once more. The truck's engine whines as it ascends the road leading out of the canyon. Then it is still.

I wander among the graves again. Gonzales is the most prevalent surname, something I had not noticed earlier. When I return to the car I consult the index to my historical atlas. There is a listing for Los Fuertes but nothing for La Cañada. The symbol next to Los Fuertes on the map identifies it as the site of a historic ruin, located upstream from San Augustín.

The sun is low on the horizon as I leave San Augustín. After crossing the river I look in vain for a road leading upstream. But I spot tire tracks heading off where the road curves up and out of the valley. They lead to a primitive road that runs along the west side of the narrow canyon. About a mile upstream the floodplain broadens again and the river bends and cuts across the valley. I stop in front of a metal gate with a No Trespassing sign. Before me, on the opposite bank, stands a concentration of stone ruins facing southeast. Gal-

vanized barbed wire tautly strung on metal posts encloses them. Sleek cattle, Santa Gertrudis stock, graze at the edge of the ruins. A bull in the field beyond bellows and strains against the fence.

I overcome my reluctance to enter posted land and squeeze through the gate. With one eye on the bull, I wade across the river and walk to the flagstone ruins. They surround a small plaza. Around them I can make out the outlines of small corrals and storage sheds. Stone fences extend north and east from the river to the canyon walls. I search the perimeter for a burial ground. None exists. There is not even a stone wall marking such a space, and not for lack of building material.

The drawn-out whistle of a locomotive interrupts the quiet, followed by the rumbling of railroad cars moving along the track. The canyon walls amplify the sounds originating upstream, producing the sensation that the train is making its way downstream and is just around the bend of the river.

I leave reluctantly but hurriedly. The sun has dropped below the horizon.

I have to ford the river once again and then successfully navigate the tracks before dark. The bull follows me along the fence all the way to the river. I turn my car around and carefully make my way back to the road, then head out of the canyon.

Just before I reach the canyon rim, I stop at a point overlooking Los Fuertes. The ruins are visible below even as dusk closes in. Sections of high wall surround the remains of smaller structures. Los Fuertes was clearly a fortified community.

As I stand in the fading light, it occurs to me that my curiosity about Papá Albino and Los Valles de San Augustín has been superficial. My brief encounter provokes more substantial questions. How did he and his family end up living on the frontier, away from the relative comfort and security of Santa Fe or the Hispano communities on the Rio Grande or its tributaries? What accounted for his literacy, given that he grew up in a rural area considerably removed from the population centers—Las Vegas, Taos, Santa Fe—where schooling would have been available? What was his experience in Los Valles de San Augustín? What moved my great-grandfather to break with his historical Roman Catholic Hispano community and convert to Protestantism? What led to his decision to abandon Los Valles de San Augustín and relocate to Las Vegas? What was his subsequent experience, and that of his siblings and offspring? And, most important, what happened to that vital community? I have seen it shrink over my lifetime. The churches of my youth are principally populated by persons even older than me. In the absence of youthful replacements, retired Hispano ministers take turns in ministering to the various flocks.

At the summit the sun still shines. The prairie meadows from which Las Vegas takes its name stretch to the north. Upstream, already in the shadow of the Sangre de Cristo Mountains, is Las Vegas; to the west, still bathed in the late afternoon sun, is Santa Fe; and to the east, out in the llano below the Canadian Escarpment, is La Trementina. The answers to my many questions lie in these communities.

INTERLOPERS

††† The tombstones surrounding Old Pine Presbyterian Church are made of granite and marble. Although harder and longer lasting than flagstone, the older ones among them are splitting, flaking, eroding away. Many have sunk into the earth. The roots of firs and sycamores have dislodged others. Unlike the camposanto in San Augustín, the burial ground surrounding the church is neatly kept. The grass and ivy are trimmed, and white and yellow crocuses line the walks. Dainty blue and lavender flowers dot the ground cover. Sleek gray squirrels search for food among the gravestones. The dogwoods are in full flower on this gray but mild late March afternoon.

My spiritual ancestors are buried in this Philadelphia cemetery, the persons who established the base for Calvinism in the New World and sought to propagate it among peoples who preceded them on the American continent. I don't recognize the names on the gravestones, but their bona fides are imposing. Buried here are Dr. John Ewing, first provost of the University of Pennsylvania and pastor of the First Presbyterian Church for forty years, and his wife, Hannah Sergeant (d. 1806); Sarah Ewing (1761–1830), wife of John Hall, marshal of Pennsylvania, and her brother, Sam Ewing (1776–1825); Major Joseph Prowere of Washington's Army (d. 1805); and Major David Lenox of the Revolutionary Army (d. 1828).

Although obtaining a Ph.D. in Spanish language and literature required me to do archival work, I did not like it or keep at it. Classrooms and boardrooms, not archives, are my preferred institutional space. Not so for the historian Antonia I. Castañeda, my spouse, at whose suggestion I began my exploration of the Hispano Protestant experience and to whose guidance and encouragement I owe my findings. While I, not unlike my students, explore the archival indexes and conclude that there is nothing available on the subject, Antonia finds the proper referent and secures the appropriate folder.

Among the holdings of the Presbyterian Historical Society, located next to

the cemetery, are the minutes of the session of the Spanish Presbyterian Church of Las Vegas, New Mexico, from November 1884 to May 1890. The ledger they are recorded in is fast deteriorating, but the entries are still legible. The third entry consists of the minutes of a worship service held in the Spanish Presbyterian Church of Las Vegas on December 21, 1888. Albino Madrid and his brother Pablo, as well as Pablo's daughter Ysidora, "were baptized and all admitted to the Lord's table" on that date. Pablo's son Manuel is listed as a student at the Las Vegas Presbyterian Mission School.

An entry for February 28, 1889, lists fourteen persons who presented themselves for baptism and admission at an evening worship service held in Los Valles de Augustín. Two of Papá Albino's offspring—Antonio and Susana—are among those received into the fellowship. My grandfather Teófilo presented himself for membership in the Las Vegas church on March 10, 1889. The entry for May 12, 1890, lists the members who "were dismissed . . . to unite to the Los Balles [*sic*] Presbyterian Church." Albino Madrid and his brother Pablo head the roll of thirty-seven individuals who form the church there. The minutes record some sixty-plus persons who figure in the membership rolls of the two Presbyterian churches established in Los Valles de San Augustín. In addition to numerous Madrids, the minutes include multiple Bleas, Estradas, Gallegos, Gonzales, Jaramillos, Luceros, and Mestas, all *protestante* names familiar to me. They are among the earliest New Mexican Hispano converts to Calvinism and share a label—*conversos*—with an earlier set of converts to Christianity: the Jewish *conversos* of fifteenth- and sixteenth-century Spain.

LONG BEFORE my ancestors became heretics, they were interlopers. My maternal ancestors, named Barela-Jaramillo, were part of the founding colony of San Gabriel de los Españoles, which was established in 1598 at the confluence of the Rio Grande and the Rio Chama, across from the indigenous community of Ohkay Owingeh, modern-day San Juan Pueblo, in what is today known as the Española Valley. They came north from the silver mining district of Zacatecas and arrived on horseback, indicative of their social standing. Like their predecessors, the *españoles* who imposed themselves on Mexico in the first half of the sixteenth century, they came in search of mineral riches.

The initial settlements on the upper Rio Grande Valley stood side by side with the communities of sedentary indigenous groups who came to be known as Pueblo Indians and even, as was the case with the capital of the kingdom, La Villa Real de la Santa Fe, on the site of a long-abandoned pueblo. As a child and teenager I spent many summers, most holidays, and many weekends on my maternal grandparents' farm in San Pedro, located across the Rio Grande from one of those indigenous villages, Kwa'po, current-day Santa Clara Pueblo. Despite its physical proximity, Santa Clara was a world apart. Except for attending festivities during their annual saint's day, and then only occasionally, we had no contact with that world. We were neighbors, lived side by side, but we saw each other infrequently and rarely engaged.

The Madrid from whom virtually all New Mexicans bearing that name are descended is listed on the expedition roll of a wagon train bringing supplies to San Gabriel from Zacatecas in 1603. His name is Francisco, and he is eight years old. His role is that of *chirrionero de carretas*, the person responsible for greasing the oxcart wheels. But unlike my maternal ancestors, Francisco walked.

The communities that the Spanish-Mexican colonizers established *río arriba*, upstream on the Rio Grande, are known to this day by one of their defining features: the plaza, the open area fronting the church. In the vicinity of the plazas were their private holdings, and surrounding them were the lands they used for pasture and as a source of fuel and building materials, to be held communally and in perpetuity. Central to a community's organization was the excavation of an irrigation system with an *acequia madre*, a "mother" irrigation ditch, to provide water to all. And, of course, every community had its camposanto, the consecrated burial ground.

When the colonizers failed to find ready riches they fell back on agriculture and stock raising to sustain themselves. They depended in large measure on the labor of their Pueblo neighbors, who reacted to abuse and exploitation by revolting against their oppressors toward the end of the seventeenth century. The colonists fled downstream with their families to take refuge in the environs of modern-day El Paso, where they remained for twelve years.

Madrids and Barelas were among the colonists who survived the Great Pueblo Revolt of 1680, the first successful uprising of indigenous peoples against the Spanish Empire. Francisco Madrid's son, also named Francisco, and his grandson Roque figure prominently in the records of punitive expeditions against the nomads who raided the El Paso colony during that period. Both father and son, along with my maternal ancestors, were among the small number of settlers who made their way upstream again to the Rio Arriba when Diego de Vargas retook New Mexico for the Spanish crown in 1692. Roque Madrid served as one of Vargas's captains. As part of the reoccupation of New Mexico in 1692, subsequently renamed a heroic *reconquista*, Francisco II led a party west to the Zuni pueblos to rescue one of his sisters, who had been taken captive during the uprising.

During the seventeenth and most of the eighteenth centuries the Hispano population was small enough to reside on the banks of the Rio Grande and its immediate environs. Nomadic indigenous groups—Apaches, Comanches, Navajos, and Utes—discouraged them from populating the lands to the north, east, or west. They raided Hispano and Pueblo settlements periodically, taking livestock, food stores, and captives. In 1705 Roque Madrid led a military force composed of Hispano settlers and Pueblo residents deep into the *cajafuerte*, the stronghold of the Apaches de Navajo, as the Navajos were then called, to punish them for their depredations. He wrote a journal about that campaign, which took him north and west into the farthest reaches of the Rio Arriba, to lands that I would subsequently call home.

Population growth during the second half of the eighteenth century forced the Hispano colonists out of their *querencias*, the secure communities of the Rio Grande basin, and drove them both upstream and downstream to the edges of their inhabited world. The first settlers of the periphery were *genízaros*—detribalized members of indigenous groups and Hispanos rescued after being brought up in captivity by those same groups—and their families. The *genízaro* settlements served as buffers against raids and as spaces where trade between the Hispano, Pueblo, and the various nomadic indigenous populations could take place. Some of those plazas have survived—Abiquiú, San Miguel del Vado, Tomé, Villanueva—and remain vital Hispano communities to this day. Others are semideserted or seasonally occupied. By the beginning of the nineteenth century, however, the settlers who went into the periphery to take possession of land grants deeded to them by the crown, and subsequently by the recently established Republic of Mexico, were the landless descendants of the original colonizers.

RIO ARRIBA

† † † I grew up two mountain ranges, three river valleys, and multiple land grants away from Las Vegas, my father's ancestral community. The village I continue to think of as home, Tierra Amarilla, is located on the upper Rio Chama Valley of north-central New Mexico. Settled in the 1860s, just after the United States occupied the area and created the Territory of New Mexico, the

village of Tierra Amarilla became (and continues to be) the governmental seat of a county larger in area than the state of Connecticut. The county carries the name that the upper Rio Grande watershed was historically known by, the Rio Arriba, which distinguished it from the lower Rio Grande watershed, the Rio Abajo.

My parents were not natives to the upper Rio Chama Valley. They had their familial roots in other Rio Arriba localities. Their religious beliefs and cultural practices, moreover, were different from those of the locals. They were Hispano Protestants in a Hispano Catholic community, and the only ones at that. The other Protestants were Anglos, either Southern Baptists or Northern Presbyterians. The subject of our religious affiliation, however, was not touched on publicly. By virtue of their professions—he an educator, she a public official—my parents had standing in our community. They may have been heretics, even interlopers, but they were treated with courtesy and respect. As a child and adolescent I was aware of that differing social status, but I had no par-

ticular sense of where it originated or what it consisted of, nor what price my parents and their parents had paid to acquire it. I did, however, know that we were different from the people of our community. We were *protestantes*, did not have the same beliefs or practices as our neighbors, were in fact set apart from them by our religious affiliation. It was an identity I took great pride in, notwithstanding my ignorance of its historical or social meaning.

My world oscillated between Tierra Amarilla and my maternal grandparents' farm in San Pedro, downstream on the east bank of the Rio Grande, a few miles south of the original colonial settlement. The sixty-five-mile trip involved a descent of some 2,000 feet and took us through stands of Douglas firs and Ponderosa pines, by slopes covered with scrub oak, around tablelands with piñon and juniper, across sagebrush and cactus ranges, and along the bluffs and buttes of the Piedra Lumbre before entering the lower Rio Chama Valley, lined with willows and cottonwoods.

U.S. Highway 84 passed through and by small ranching and farming communities, most of which bore descriptive names: Las Nutrias, though the otters had disappeared long ago; La Cebolla, for the wild onions that grew along its creek; Barranca, marking the gorge at the entrance to the lower Rio Chama Valley; Medanales, for its neighboring sand dunes; Tierra Azul, for the blue-green tints in the adjacent foothills; La Cuchilla, referring to the knifelike geological formation above the settlement; El Duende, the dwarf, contracted from San Francisco el Duende. The origins of other names along the route—Abiquiú, Chilí, El Guache—were likely corruptions of indigenous names whose meanings are lost to history. And finally there was Española, the collective name that came into use late in the nineteenth century for the Spanish-Mexican colonial settlements—San Pedro, Santa Cruz, Santo Niño—located at the confluence of the Rio Grande and the Rio Santa Cruz.

Twice yearly, when I was a child, either over the Thanksgiving or Christmas holidays and at some point during the summer, my father drove us south and east from Tierra Amarilla to visit his mother and siblings. The semiannual journeys to Las Vegas offered different terrains and other place-names. Still familiar to me, though we didn't travel it as frequently, was the road to Santa Fe, which went past communities with Puebloan names—Nambé, Pojoaque, Cuyamungué, Tesuque.

Outside Santa Fe, Highway 84 wound its way east through the foothills along the route of the Old Santa Fe Trail and dropped into Apache Canyon. At the bottom of the canyon the roadway and the tracks of the Santa Fe Railroad meet and run parallel to each other along the route of the Santa Fe Trail up through Glorieta Pass and into the Pecos River Valley. The only communities between the pass and the river are two railroad fueling stops, each with their water and coal towers: Ilfeld and Rowe. On occasion we sighted a locomotive refueling, but the sooty railroad structures were not as interesting as the ruins of the Pecos Mission to the north or the butte known as Starvation Peak looming on the eastern horizon.

I was, however, curious about the names of those two sites along the highway. Except for the unimaginative labels—Park View, Riverside, Fairview—overlaid on some Rio Arriba communities, the place-names of my home territory were Spanish or Puebloan. But Ilfeld and Rowe were the names of people. Charles Ilfeld Mercantile Company trucks delivered goods to the small grocery stores found in every community of the Rio Arriba. Charles Ilfeld, my father said, was a wealthy landowner and a member of the infamous Santa Fe Ring, a group of businesspeople and politicians who dispossessed Hispanos of their communal lands. And Rowe, he added, was a railroad contractor who helped introduce the railroad into New Mexico at the end of the nineteenth century.

The highway and railroad crossed the Pecos River just north of San Miguel del Vado and turned north some ten miles later. The railroad bed, like the wagon trail, followed the contours of the land, weaving around knolls and bluffs, but the highway cut through the foothills and across the Tecolote River Valley. Only the anticipation of arriving at my maternal grandmother's home attenuated the sadness I felt as we drove through the arid landscape and past the tiny riverine communities of Bernal and Tecolote. The landscape and villages were not unlike those we traversed between Tierra Amarilla and San Pedro, but these, I felt, were *tristes*—sad and pitiful. Little did I appreciate that my feelings were informed by those of my parents, particularly my father's. He did not have good memories from his adolescence or young adulthood. Las Vegas was not a place he recalled fondly. And my mother had her own reasons for disliking Las Vegas, which I would in time come to appreciate.

The highway and railway converged at a narrow gap at Romeroville, emerging into the vast meadowlands from which Las Vegas takes its name. As we exited the gap and entered the open prairie, my father invariably pointed with his chin toward the east and said, "*De allí era mi abuelo, Papá Albino.*" The *allí* was Los Valles de San Augustín, located somewhere in what seemed to me, who had grown up in a valley surrounded by mountains and hills, an endless horizon. Even when I was a child the name struck a chord. It had biblical resonance. It conjured up vastness and plentitude. And it was associated with a legendary name: Albino Madrid, my father's grandfather, a blacksmith and silversmith by trade, who sometime in the late nineteenth century traded his *abecedario*—his spelling book—for a Bible, converted to Protestantism, and moved upstream to Las Vegas to join his new community of faith.

My father told about sitting and listening to Papá Albino as he worked in his blacksmith shop. Papá Albino, Dad said, was a learned man, who told him stories from the Old Testament and *The Arabian Nights*. Papá Albino also read to him from fin-de-siècle Spanish novels, including *The Four Horsemen of the Apocalypse* by Vicente Blasco Ibáñez, which he later studied in college and saw made into a Hollywood movie starring Rudolph Valentino. By the time I went to college I not only knew the Old Testament stories; I had also read my father's collection of late nineteenth- and early twentieth-century Spanish novels, an intellectual legacy passed down by my great-grandfather Albino.

What most stands out in my mind is my father's recollection that on summer evenings Papá Albino liked to argue politics and religion with the other denizens of the Old Town plaza. That memory has served me well in moments of political and social conflict. His learning and his faith were his *fuerte*, a mighty fortress that provided him armor for his daily struggles with ethnic rejection and religious enmity.

LOS VALLES DE SAN AUGUSTÍN

† † † I first visited San Augustín in the company of my father, Arturo Teófilo, and my son, Raúl Lorca, a century and a half after the valley was settled. We turned off the interstate, the latter-day version of the Santa Fe Trail, just south of Las Vegas. The all-weather road that forks off from the highway parallels the Gallinas River, which flows in a southeasterly direction from its source in the Sangre de Cristo Mountains, dividing Las Vegas into Old Town and New Town. Below Las Vegas the river cuts a deep canyon into the plateau. The course of the river is evident only because of the piñon and juniper trees that grow along the canyon rim. As it makes its way down into the northern edge of the Llano Estacado, the name Spanish explorers gave to the southwestern Great Plains, the canyon opens into cultivable if narrow valleys known collectively as Los Valles de San Augustín.

Along a ten-mile stretch of the river lie the remains of various nineteenth-century communities established as part of the Las Vegas Grandes Community Land Grant of 1835. While some of these settlements—San Augustín, Chaperito, La Concepción, La Liendre—are still listed on road maps and can sometimes be found on road markers, they are principally ranch sites and mostly uninhabited. The existence of still others, however—Ojito, Lourdes, El Aguila, Los Fuertes, Los Torres—is recorded only in the memories of the living or in documents left by the departed.

The gravel road leading off the freeway, surveyor-straight and passably maintained by the county, is bounded on both sides by taut woven wire strung on metal posts. No Trespassing signs and metal sheets signaling membership in the New Mexico Cattleman's Association hang from the fences. Ranch entrances are marked by elaborate gates bearing their names, as well as cattle guards. Prairie meadow gradually gives way to piñon and juniper trees. The all-weather road ends at the canyon rim, replaced by a rutted dirt road. A handcrafted sign announces that one is entering the Las Vegas Grandes Land Grant. The galvanized woven wire is replaced by rusty barbed wire strung on cedar posts.

From the lip of the canyon formed by the Gallinas River as it intersects with a large dry wash, we looked over the long-lot fields bisecting the floodplain and the adjoining banks. An irrigation ditch followed the river's eastern contours, feeding the orchards and alfalfa fields below it. The floodplain was meadowland, and the west bank served as pasture. The settlement of San Augustín was visible on the eastern riverbank above the floodplain. It consisted of a dozen or so buildings and ruins, with attendant sheds and animal pens. Dusty-looking Chinese elms shaded the dwellings.

The dirt road leading into the valley cuts into the canyon and winds along its contours. Huge sandstone boulders, some larger than a passenger van, sit precariously on both sides of the road. The drop from the plateau to the river bottom is considerable, some 500 feet. A concrete platform bridges the river just below the dam that diverts its waters

into a cottonwood-lined irrigation ditch. Beside the ditch, and between it and a sandstone cliff, lies San Augustín, an assemblage of stone buildings, chinked and plastered with adobe, topped by pitched, zinc-covered roofs; verandas with benches situated along the wall of the dwellings; fenced yards, within which grew hollyhocks, lilacs, and rose bushes; and all around us the accumulated leavings of a century and a half—ancient farm equipment, outmoded kitchen appliances, discarded containers of all sizes and shapes. No one was around, although we could smell piñon wood burning.

The village cemetery is situated on a slope to the east of the settlement. Most of the gravestones are severely eroded, but on some we could make out markings. Scratched into the soft flagstone native to the area were the words *finó*—from *finar*, to come to the end—or *falleció*—from *fallecer*, to expire—followed by names and dates. My father scanned the tombstones for ones bearing his surname, and when he found one read it out loud to us: Preciliano Madrid, *falleció el 18 de julio de 1905*; María Bonifacia Madrid (no date) opposite J. Hilario García, *falleció este 14 de diciembre de 1898*; M.g MDA Madrid, *finó septiembre 1 de 1887*; and Demetrio Madrid, *falleció este día 29 de diciembre de 1890*. He did not recognize the names.

EL CERRITO AND LAS VEGAS GRANDES

† † † "Dr. Madrid, have you met Richard Nostrand?" archivist Al Regensberger asks as I enter the New Mexico State Archives, where I have been poring over census records. I have not had any success tracing Papá Albino's trajectory. The 1845 census of the Departamento de Nuevo México lists one José Albino Madrid, age eight, son of José Antonio and Petra Mestas, residents of Bayes (*sic*) de San Augustín. The next entry is Rafael Madrid, whom I assume is José Antonio's father. The 1827 census lists a José Antonio in the household of Rafael Madrid, a resident of Santa Fe, which seems to confirm the relation.

A noted cultural geographer, Nostrand is the author of *The Hispano Homeland*, one of my principal guides to New Mexico. He is in Santa Fe carrying out research before classes start at the University of Oklahoma. "Madrid," he says. "That's one of the families who lived in El Cerrito, the village I'm studying." Intrigued, I ask him their names. "Rafael, and his son José Antonio," he answers to my great delight. I tell him that José Antonio is Rafael's son by his second wife, María Manuela Saiz, and father to Albino Madrid. Nostrand is equally pleased. He has not been able to work out the full genealogy.

Nostrand has an 1841 census taken by the Departamento de Nuevo México that I have not seen. It records my ancestors as residents of the valley of El Cerrito. In the decade after Mexico obtained its independence from Spain, Rafael Madrid moved his family downstream and east from La Villa Real de la Santa Fe to the eastern edge of the Hispano world. Papá Albino's grandfather was not among the landholding families of El Cerrito, but his second wife, María

Manuela Saiz, was aunt to one of the principal landowning settlers, which explained his presence in that village. Papá Albino is listed as being age four and the son of José Antonio Madrid and Petra Mestas. His brother Pablo is three years old.

"Where is El Cerrito?" I ask. Nostrand shows me a map. It is downstream from San Miguel del Vado, on the Pecos River, just beyond Villanueva. Nostrand tells me he has fallen in love with the village, has even bought a house there. I had visited the lower Pecos River Valley early in my explorations, knowing that it was a steppingstone for the settlers who moved out into the llano, but I was unaware of El Cerrito's existence.

Villanueva sits on a steep bluff overlooking the Pecos at the point where it bends due east. Its location and layout indicate that it was a *fuerte*, a fortified community. The adobe dwellings are built cheek to cheek and face inward into a large plaza. At its center is the church, a large and solid structure with a stone façade. Its style—French Provincial, introduced into the New Mexico Territory by Jean-Baptiste Lamy, the French-born archbishop sent by the American Catholic Church to counter the proselytizing efforts of the Protestants—belies its building materials: adobe brick.

Mariano Baros and José Felipe Madrid founded Villanueva in 1809. The name Isidora Saiz de Madrid is inscribed on the largest and most prominent headstone in its churchyard. In a more prestigious location, inside the nave, lie the remains of José Felipe and his descendants, none of whom figure in the familial genealogy I have constructed.

My childhood friend Alfonso, now a resident of Santa Fe, owns a high-center SUV. He is always ready to explore new places and revisit old ones. Unlike my father, he is disposed to make stops along the way. We set off east and north from Santa Fe on I-25 in July and exit shortly to visit the church at Cañoncito. The interstate crowds it, robbing it of any perspective on its magnificent setting, the reddish canyon walls of Apache Canyon. A few miles later we make an illegal stop on the side of the interstate to examine an eccentric, private monument marking the Union forces' decisive victory over the Confederacy for control of the New Mexico Territory. Curiously, no official monument exists. We continue over the pass and along the edge of Santa Fe National Forest toward the Pecos River. Along the river, both above and below the interstate, are small communities—San Ysidro, San José, San Juan, San Miguel.

Downstream from the communities with saintly names lie plazas with more prosaic appellations, spun off from the mother settlement of San Miguel del Vado—Sena, Ribera, La Fragua, La Puebla, and Villanueva. To the west is Glorieta Mesa, its once denuded slopes now covered by a lush growth of pine, piñon, juniper, and scrub oak. On the hills and buttes of privately held land to the east, the piñon and juniper trees are spare and stunted. Cacti, tumbleweeds, and tufts of grass sit on miniature islands carved out of the thin layer of topsoil by wind and rain.

From its source in the alpine meadows of the Pecos Wilderness, the Pecos River flows south and east on its way to the Gulf of Mexico. At the higher elevations it is a clear,

fast-running stream, urgently pushing debris out of its way. Below the town of Pecos, the runoff from cloudbursts that rushes down arroyos frequently turns the stream murky. As the Pecos descends into the llano, the riverbed widens. Its waters become warm and move slowly, as if the river has arrived safely at its destination and needs to hurry no more, even though it runs hundreds of miles more, all the way to the Rio Grande and ultimately into the Gulf.

The banks of the Pecos are the color of last season's ground red chile, as is the plaster on the adobe dwellings that define the tiny settlements. When it rains, the river's waters turn a reddish chocolate color, like a thin Oaxacan mole sauce. Ancient cottonwoods, wild plum bushes, and ivy grow along the acequia that feeds the meadows, diminutive orchards, and even smaller garden plots enclosed in the long-lot fields intersecting the floodplain.

Just below Villanueva the valley narrows into an impassable gorge, then opens up a few miles downstream. El Cerrito is located in a small hollow formed by a bend in the river before it closes up again. It is accessible only by ascending the bluff opposite Villanueva and descending it some seven miles later. We drive along a county all-weather road that provides right-of-way through privately held land. To the south the llano extends with its infinite horizon; to the east and west rise the mesas that flank the Pecos. To the north we can see the tip of the pointed butte known as Starvation Peak, and beyond it the foothills of the Sangre de Cristo range.

Viewed from the edge of the bluff, El Cerrito is an oasis. The settlement is nestled against the northwest end of the hollow. It is a tiny valley, less than fifty acres in size. The arable land, along the north bank of the river, lies uncultivated. The pastures of the llano, the woodlands on the mesas and its flanks, and the waters of the Pecos would have recommended the valley to its settlers, despite its size.

We descend slowly down a rutted roadway. Small orchards crowd the settlement—apple trees, mainly ancient, with an occasional pear tree. The houses are constructed out of the area's abundant flagstone and plastered over with adobe. Most are in ruins, but some are being reconstructed. I wonder aloud which one belongs to Richard Nostrand, which requires me to tell Alfonso the full story. The houses surround a small plaza with a small capilla in the middle that faces south. We park and enter the churchyard. Hollyhocks line the front. They are my favorite color, wine red highlighted by a pale yellow stamen. A hand-carved sign above the entry door reads "Nuestra Señora de los Desamparados," Our Lady of the Luckless.

I am conscious of being watched. The men working on a neighboring house, one of whom is repairing the roof, have interrupted their work. Two young boys wander over to take a closer look at us. I leave Alfonso to explore the churchyard and approach the man on the ground. He wears a western-style straw hat, jeans, and work boots. We share the same coloring, but his skin is weather-beaten. "*Buenos días. Andamos conociendo*," I say. The dance is always the same: I explain that my family lived here; he asks their name; I provide it;

he tells me there are no Madrids in the community, that he has no memory of anyone by that name. I ask about the cemetery. He motions east with his chin. I ask about the residents. Making a face, he explains that there are only a few locals. Most are like him, he tells me, summer residents who come from Colorado, Utah, and Wyoming to see to their ancestral holdings. I ask him for Richard Nostrand's house. Over there, he indicates, again with his chin. Like many of the others, the house is in an advanced state of deterioration, but someone has been attending to it. Wood is stacked on the porch, the weeds have been trimmed, and the window screens are in place.

We loiter briefly in the churchyard, take pictures of the plaza, then head northeast toward Starvation Peak and on to Los Valles de San Augustín via a primitive road that leads us to Bernal and the interstate.

El Cerrito proved too small to accommodate the Madrid family, and they soon moved farther into the eastern frontier, to a land grant authorized by the Mexican government in 1836. Known as Las Vegas Grandes, the grant included grasslands extending as far as the eye could see. It was located on the eastern slopes of the southern Rocky Mountains, at the western end of the Great American Prairie, on lands that had been home to the Jicarilla Apache and that subsequently sheltered Comanches and Kiowas.

The settlers of Las Vegas Grandes were a reluctant group. They were attracted by the prospects of vast meadowlands (*vegas*) to pasture their sheep on, ample water for their crops, extensive woodlands (*montes*) to meet their building and fuel needs, and plentiful deer, wild turkeys—known to them as *gallinas de la tierra*—and, if they were inclined to venture into the llano, the westernmost edge of the Great Plains, bison. Apaches, Comanches, and Kiowas, however, were still a threat when the first permanent settlement was established on the banks of the Gallinas River. To defend themselves against raiding parties, the Hispano settlers of Las Vegas Grandes built *fuertes*, clustering their homes around the community plaza for mutual defense. Raids against the settlers continued unabated into the second half of the century. Apaches took Andrés Martínez, a ten-year-old Hispano, captive while he was tending livestock on family holdings near Las Vegas in 1844. Andrés escaped and was taken in by a Kiowa band, but he did not return to New Mexico until he was an adult. He recorded his life in a memoir titled *Andele*, the name he had as a Kiowa.

The 1845 census of the Departamento de Nuevo México, a province of the República de México, gives official status to the lower Gallinas River Valley, registering it as Los Bayes (*sic*) de San Augustín. It was part of the parish of San Miguel del Vado. Among its residents is José Albino, who lives with his parents, José Antonio Madrid and Petra Mestas. Albino's age is recorded as eight years—that is, only two years younger than his neighbor Andrés Martínez.

THE INCIDENT AT LOS VALLES

† † † "Los Valles, Los Valles . . . hmm. There was an incident at that place, shortly after the occupation of New Mexico," Roberto Torres tells me. "Some members of the U.S. Army of the West were found dead nearby. I think there's a military record." Torres is the New Mexico state historian. We grew up in adjacent villages in the upper Rio Chama Valley, I in Tierra Amarilla, he a few miles farther north in Los Ojos.

In 1846, on his way to California, Stephen B. Kearny, the commanding general of the U.S. Army of the West, assembled the populace of Las Vegas, the first *nuevomexicano* community he occupied, and announced: "We come as friends, to better your condition. . . . My government . . . will keep off the Indians, protect you in your persons and property and . . . will protect you in your religion." Although it was subsequently characterized as a "bloodless conquest," the occupation of New Mexico had violent dimensions. The residents of Los Valles de San Augustín, despite the valley's isolation, experienced the violence that accompanied the military takeover.

In 1847 an abortive rebellion in Taos resulted in the death of Charles Bent, New Mexico's first U.S. governor. A few months later raiders took horses belonging to the Missouri Volunteers, part of the U.S. military force based in Las Vegas. An officer and two enlisted men, accompanied by a Hispano volunteer, were dispatched to follow the missing horses' trail. They apparently found the animals in Los Valles, and when they attempted to recover them they were set upon and killed. In retaliation a cavalry force attacked the village on July 5, killing twelve residents in the process. The corpses of the enlisted men and the volunteer had been incinerated, but the officer's body was found nearby, spared, it is speculated, because he was wearing a cross. A search of the residences turned up clothes, equipment, and personal items belonging to the deceased. The commanding officer, concluding on that basis that the entire

community was party to the theft of the horses and the death of the soldiers, burned the residences to the ground, save for some dwellings set aside to provide shelter to the women and children. The soldiers took the men prisoner and marched them fifty-some miles to Santa Fe.

According to the only known official record of the event, the proceedings of a court-martial held in late July, five of the prisoners were found guilty of murder and executed on August 3. Oral tradition has it that the remaining prisoners were whipped before being released, but that is not part of the official record. The historian Marc Simmons writes that shortly thereafter the residents abandoned the settlement, moved half a mile downstream, and founded San Augustín. If that is the case, the incident took place at the site that subsequently came to be known as Los Fuertes.

Curiously, neither Albino nor his parents or siblings are listed in the first official U.S. Census of the newly annexed territory, taken in 1850. Not in Los

Valles de San Augustín, in any of the neighboring communities, or anywhere in the Territory of New Mexico. Albino Madrid would have been thirteen years old at the time of the census; his brother Pablo would have been eleven. Their grandfather, Rafael Madrid, however, is recorded as a resident of Las Vegas, which may have included Los Valles de San Augustín, since the place-names of the other settlements on the Gallinas River do not figure in the 1850 census.

Was Albino's father, José Antonio, one of the twelve killed in the attack? Or, given the nature of their previous encounter with representatives of the new society, did they eschew contact with the census taker? No one by the name of Madrid is listed in the records of the court-martial held in Santa Fe in July 1847 or is in any way implicated in the incident at Los Valles. And there is no familial memory of that traumatic event nor any stories connected to it.

Albino Madrid reappears ten years later in the 1860 Territorial Census of New Mexico, which lists him as a resident of Los Valles de San Augustín. Not so his father, José Antonio. Listed as part of Albino's household are his mother, Petra Mestas, and two younger brothers—Lázaro and Bonifacio. Grandfather Albino is married to Juana Baca. They have one son, Pedro. Albino's occupation is listed as blacksmith. The census indicates that he is literate.

LORENZO GONZALES, EL GÜERO

† † † "*Buenas tardes*," I say to the driver of a half-ton Chevy pickup loaded with hay who stops next to our vehicle. I am in the company of friends, Estevan Rael-Gálvez, the newly appointed New Mexico state historian, and Juan Ríos, a public official, videographer, and former television reporter. Estevan wants to learn more about the Hispano Protestants, who do not figure in New Mexico's master narrative. Juan is intrigued by the story of my encounter with the Marlboro Man and hopes to film us meeting for a second time.

We are looking down on Los Valles de San Augustín from the bluff at the rim of the canyon. It is just after lunch on a day in late July. The cumulus clouds are beginning to float over the Sangre de Cristo Mountains and skim across the prairie sky. The rain earlier in the week has provided enough moisture to infuse the air with the odor of piñon resin, and a few cicadas intone the first notes of what will become a monotonous symphony.

"*Buenas tardes*," the man in the truck answers in kind. Motioning at Juan's video camera with his chin, he asks, "*¿Qué hacen?*" My family was from the area, I tell him. We're filming for a story about them. I introduce my companions and myself. "Rosendo Gonzales," he responds, then tells us other film crews have come to the area over the years. There is disapproval in his tone. Their stories, he says, bring unwanted attention to the valley, and despoilers.

We commiserate. I know about the depredations of outsiders. They have stripped La Trementina's ruins of building stone. I reaffirm the personal nature of our project, then tell him of my previous visits and of meeting the Marlboro Man, who recommended that I talk to Lorenzo Gonzales.

"*Son mis hermanos*," Rosendo says. The Marlboro Man is his youngest brother, Arturo. Lorenzo is the oldest of his siblings. Rosendo wears a weather-beaten Stetson whose original color is unclear. He has a lighter complexion than his younger brother Arturo, but the elements have been hard on his skin. Motioning toward San Augustín, he tells us to visit Lorenzo, El Güero, who has all the stories. "*Está haciendo chicos,*" he says, laughing. "*Chicos*," Estevan exclaims. "Hardly anyone makes them anymore." *Chicos* are made from fresh corn that is roasted, set out to dry, and husked. It is a highly nutritional, much valued foodstuff particular to New Mexico.

After his departure we continue to look down on the valley. Estevan, the anthropologist and historian, grins and says, "We're interloping. We're outsiders looking in." But he is no outsider. Although still a young man and only recently appointed to his post, he is widely known. And he fits in. His elongated, elegant face mirrors the images of the Christs and saints found on the *retablos* and *bultos* of eighteenth-century New Mexico. Unlike Juan and me, in our khakis, guayaberas, and casual shoes, he wears boots, jeans, and fitted shirts. The only item he lacks is the Stetson favored by ranchers young and old.

After making our way slowly down the canyon to the village, we park in the large plaza in front of the San Augustín chapel. Juan opens the back door of his SUV and takes out his camera equipment. Estevan and I head for the chapel. As we cross the plaza we hear a voice calling to us from a house located to the north of the chapel. I see a man standing in the front yard. He is waving to us. "I have to go over," I say to Estevan. He nods. Like me, he was brought up in northern New Mexico; he, too, enters rural spaces cautiously.

I approach the yard and call out, "*Buenas tardes*." "*Buenas tardes*," the man responds. He is in his late sixties or early seventies, about five and a half feet tall, my height but heavier by some thirty pounds, and, despite his sun-ravaged skin, of fair complexion. He wears a weathered cowboy hat made of straw. His eyes are light green, and his graying sideburns have a reddish tint. He is quite obviously El Güero, the light-skinned one, recommended to me by Gimme Cap a decade before.

I hasten to explain ourselves, beginning with my familial connections to Los Valles de San Augustín. "*¿Cómo se llamaban?*" El Güero wants to know. "Madrid," I answer. "*¿Cuándo van a volver los Madriles?*" "Pardon?" I say, puzzled. He repeats his question. "Who?" I stammer. "*Los Madriles*," he says. They visited many years ago, he explains. A man in a wheelchair and his father. In a van. They said they would return, but they never have. "Ah," I say, still surprised but now understanding. It would have been my father and my brother Ibáñez, a quadriplegic. I explain that they are both deceased. He mumbles his condolences.

We stand there quietly, he and I, protected from the glare of the afternoon sun by the Chinese elms surrounding the yard. El Güero is holding a can of beer in one hand. In the other is an ear of corn. His face is flushed, and he is a bit unsteady. There are three other persons in the yard, a man and two women. The women are bent over tubs on the veranda, and the man is stacking ears of corn in an adobe oven. They drip water as he removes them from a nearby tub. The smell of burning piñon wood and roasting corn takes me back to my childhood, to late autumn on my maternal grandparents' farm, when we shucked the corn and prepared it to make two other highly prized foodstuffs: posole, the New Mexican version of hominy, and cornmeal.

Lorenzo explains that his daughter Socorro, his nephew William, and William's wife, Benigna, are helping him prepare *chicos*. He is supervising their labors, in a manner of speaking. William continues to place ears of corn in the outdoor oven. Socorro and Benigna strip and hang the processed corn from the previous day. While Lorenzo and I are speaking my companions join me. Estevan refills the tub with ears of corn while William closes and seals the oven. Juan walks to the porch and films the women at their task.

I, however, am El Güero's captive. He wants my full attention. We are standing face to face, at a physical closeness intimidating even to me, accustomed to the intimate personal distance favored by Latinos. His left hand is wrapped around my upper arm. His grip is strong. I do not resist. But there is a price. His breath is sweet but unpleasant, both medicinal and cloying. The smell reminds me of putrefying apples. He releases me only to hitch up his trousers. Like me, he has no hips. From time to time, between pulls on his bottle, he wipes his nose on his shirtsleeve. El Güero does not offer to share his beer.

After further interrogation he says, "*Tu tío Gerónimo vivía allí*," and motions west toward some ruins. "*Pobrecito. Murió solo.*" Gerónimo Madrid, one of my Grandfather Teófilo's older siblings, lived behind the chapel, he tells me. Lorenzo would not have known my great-uncle Gerónimo, who was born in 1865 and died in 1918. Yet he talks about him familiarly and in the near past. It is clearly a familial story that he carries on. Uncle Gerónimo died alone, El

Güero says, on a very cold Christmas Eve, after a visit to Lorenzo's relations. *Pobrecito*, he says. Poor soul. It is an expression of sympathy, but it also communicates a difference in economic and social status between the speaker and his subject. Turning east he again motions with his chin, this time to a neighboring house. "*Allí vivía tu tío Porfirio*," he says. "*Era platero*." Uncle Porfirio lived next door. He fashioned rings out of silver, El Güero tells me. He looks up sorrowfully, touching his fingers. "*Pobrecito*," he repeats.

The hour is late, and we take our leave. El Güero, however, is not done with me. He wants to hear more about the filming. "Can I be in it?" he asks with an impish smile. I play along. "We'll be back soon," I say, in an effort to break away. He invites us to lunch the next day. Socorro, the daughter, makes a face. But while Lorenzo has been talking at me I have been eavesdropping on Estevan's conversation with Lorenzo's nephew, whom he knows slightly. William is member of the Las Vegas Grandes Land Grant Association, and Estevan has asked about the ruins at Los Fuertes. William offers to take us there. I accept the invitation on our behalf with alacrity. Much to Estevan's delight, as El Güero sends us off he gives us an armload of *chicos* that have been drying on the veranda.

Our brunch the next morning consists of beans with *chicos*, red chile stew, fried potatoes and eggs, and tortillas. We take turns sitting at the small kitchen table. El Güero, pleased that we have replenished his supply of beer, is less garrulous than he was the previous day. Socorro is friendlier, and in response to our compliments on the food and to the groceries we have brought she warms to our presence. After I have eaten she ushers me into the adjacent sitting room, reserved for company. It is the space of my childhood memories, one I associate with my parents' visits to pay respects to the bereaved following someone's passing. The sofa is covered with a crocheted spread. Doilies large and small adorn every possible surface. Photographs hang on the walls—an-

cient ones, oval in shape and tinted in pastel colors, black-and-white wedding portraits, and sepia-tinted pictures of men in uniform.

William shows us the house he and Benigna are refurbishing, as well as the improvements he has made in the surrounding yard. The acequia runs right by the house, and along it are young peach, apricot, and apple trees, a raspberry patch, and an arbor with a grapevine loaded with Concord grapes. But it is Los Fuertes and the camposanto I am interested in, and after a decent interval we head upstream. We stop at the concrete bridge across the Gallinas, and William shows us where the river is diverted into the acequia. He kneels and grabs a handful of mud from under the bank. He rinses the mud from his hand to reveal two large wriggling crayfish. Don't they have commercial value? I ask. "*Sí*," William says, "*pero están contaminados*." The water is polluted from untreated waste dumped upriver, in Las Vegas, he explains. I nod. Alice Blake, a turn-of-the-century Presbyterian missionary, writes in her unpublished mem-

oir that the depopulation of Los Valles de San Augustín was also prompted by polluted waters flowing downstream from Las Vegas. Not much has changed a century later.

Los Fuertes became the property of his father's grandfather at the end of the nineteenth century, William explains as we make our way upstream. "*Se lo compraron a los Madriles*," he says, confirming the Marlboro Man's story concerning his great-grandfather's purchase of land from the Madrid family. But the upper valley was lost at midcentury to a Texas land corporation and has subsequently changed owners several times. Access to the ruins of Los Fuertes, which has been designated a historic site, is required by law, notwithstanding an imposing fence and the No Trespassing signs.

We ford the stream and walk through the ruins. As we wander, William stoops and picks up a shard of pottery. He looks around and finds chips of flint. The valley, he informs us, has numerous prehistoric archaeological sites. The site Los Fuertes occupies would have been a very desirable one, providing

not only a good field of vision but also an escape route. He motions with his chin to the branch canyon leading northeast out of the valley. Up higher, at the lip of the canyon and the edge of the prairie, is a spring that provides water year-round, he tells us. A pool forms where it issues forth from the canyon. "*Le dicen el Aguaje de los Madriles*," he says. It is the watering hole Gimme Cap referred to.

I ask William about the Los Valles de San Augustín incident. "*Comancheros*," he responds. "*Eran comancheros los que se robaron la remuda militar. Pero le echaron la culpa a la gente*." In William's version the rustlers were *comancheros*, Hispanos who provided horses to the Comanche peoples in return for cattle. When it came to assessing responsibility, however, the Missouri Volunteers made no distinction between shepherds and rustlers.

We walk to the bank overlooking the Gallinas. The valley at Los Fuertes is narrow, less than 300 yards wide. The river here traverses the valley from west to east and then cuts into the bank, which rises some twenty feet above the stream before looping west again. The riverbank has been eroding for some time. I tell William that during my previous visits I looked in vain for a cemetery. Motioning west, he explains that the river's original course was across the floodplain and along the canyon wall. The fields the inhabitants of Los Fuertes had under cultivation originally extended to the riverbank on the canyon's western edge. A flood changed the river's course. The camposanto would have been in its path.

Somewhere, in some archive, I have read about a flood along the upper Gallinas River Valley in 1909. It swept away a large number of dwellings and commercial buildings upstream, along the river dividing Old Town and New Town Las Vegas. Downstream it cut through the camposanto of Los Fuertes. My ancestors' remains became part of the silt deposited along the floodplain and on the delta formed by the river as it exits the canyon and enters the llano.

LOS FUERTES

† † † A decade and a half after my first visit to Los Valles de San Augustín, I return once again, this time in the company of photographer Miguel Gandert. Intrigued by my stories and by a visit we made to Los Valles the previous fall, Miguel has proposed a series of photos to accompany my text. He specifically wants to visit Los Fuertes, which he has seen only from the lip of the canyon on a cold November day.

It is midweek in late summer, and the valley is quiet. Before we make our way upstream to Los Fuertes, we visit San Augustín. As we drive down the narrow lane between the cliff and the acequia that provides water to the adjacent fields and orchards, we see a bald eagle feasting on a heron at the far edge of a field. The heron's feathers are scattered like the plumes of mature dandelions, mute testimony to its attempt to escape the surprise attack. We stop to observe. The raptor continues to tear its prey, unbothered by our presence.

We wander about the village. Miguel shoots away. Like Lorenzo, he has a light complexion. Despite his German last name, he is a Hispano through and through, including having a *genízaro* ancestor, his maternal great-grandmother. We have struck up a fast friendship during my semester as a visiting professor at the University of New Mexico, where he holds an academic appointment. Miguel is renowned for his photographs of New Mexico, its peoples, and its practices.

Black squirrels scurry around, feasting on the ripening apples beginning to fall from the trees. In the distance we hear the bell of the herd's lead goat. The arroyo continues to cut into the camposanto. No one is around, although smoke issues from a pipe poking through one of the corrugated metal roofs.

We make our way back to the turnoff to Los Fuertes and follow the ruts upstream. A cattle gate bars our way. We leave the car on the roadbed and let ourselves in. A small residential trailer, seemingly uninhabited, is parked above the floodplain, and a smaller hitch is snuggled against the canyon wall. Neither was present during my visit two years earlier with Estevan and Juan, and there was no fence blocking access to Los Fuertes. We clamber over the fence and make our way to the river, which is running low. Miguel secures his camera equipment, hikes up his trousers, and wades through the shallow ford vehicles use to cross the river. Ever fastidious, I find a spot where I can leap from sandbar to rock to log without getting wet.

As we wander through the ruins, I fill Miguel in on what I have learned. Although I have confirmed most of the Marlboro Man's information, I still do not know where the *protestante* church and cemetery were located. William Gonzales had given me an acceptable explanation for the cemetery's absence in Los Fuertes. My cousin Carlos Trujillo had called to say that he had been told the *protestante* church still existed. But I hadn't found anyone in Los Valles who could tell me where it was.

Towering cumulus clouds drift across sky made intensely blue by the framing of the canyon walls. The river is running high after recent rains, and the vegetation along it is soft and green. We sit under an ancient cottonwood and speculate about the ruins. One of them must have been the church, Miguel suggests. We make our way toward the river. I point out the flood gauge on the opposite side, next to where the funicular used to transverse the stream when the river was running high.

As we return to the car, Miguel stops. He has spotted a bird resting atop a diminutive structure rising above the bare floodplain. We walk toward it. It is a slender piece of flagstone, partially covered by bird droppings. I pour what is left in my water bottle on it and clean the surface with my handkerchief. There are characters carved into the flagstone—an R and an M. We look around to see if there are other stones. We make none out but notice slight mounds of earth near the solitary marker. They are evenly spaced, some four feet apart, extending away from the flagstone. Despite the sun's warmth, a chill runs through me. Here most likely are the remains of what the Marlboro Man termed the *campohereje*, the burial ground of my Madrid forebears.

We ford the river once more. Miguel walks across, water up to his calves. This time I am not so fortunate, and I end up with one foot in the stream. In our excitement we have not noticed that we have company. An older man stands next to the small hitch located under the trees along the canyon wall. He is tall and gaunt, a Hispano Ichabod Crane. His jeans are faded, as is his checkered shirt, and his work boots are scuffed and worn. Except for his stained L.A. Dodgers cap, he looks like the elderly men I used to see in the plazas of the upper Rio Chama watershed. His wrinkled face and stooped stance resemble theirs. A pickup truck and attached trailer are parked nearby. I ask myself how he got past my car, which straddles the entryway.

"*Buenas tardes*," I call out as we approach the fence. He responds in kind. I perform my explanatory ritual: rationale, name, bona fides. He nods. I apologize for blocking his access. He waves it off. I introduce Miguel. "Bernardo Gonzales, *a sus órdenes*," he offers. I tell him about my contacts with the Gonzales family. He nods. "*Son mis hermanos*," he says. El Güero is the oldest of six siblings.

I comment on the fence, the gate, and the trailer. They weren't here during my last visit, I say. "I moved back two years ago," he explains. "From California, where I went in the late 1950s." I nod. Hispanos, including members of my own family, left New Mexico in search of employment during those difficult years. "I retired and wanted to come back. My wife didn't. She stayed behind. I fenced off the property I inherited from my father and brought a trailer in. I live here until it gets too cold in my trailer or the road is becoming impassable, and then I move to Las Vegas."

As we visit, Miguel shoots away, and our host, intrigued and flattered, warms to us. What about Los Fuertes? I want to know. When was it abandoned? "One family was still living there when we moved to Las Vegas in the early 1950s," he says, "but I don't think they remained much longer. It was too cold to farm. The pasturelands on both sides of the valley had been fenced by the new Texan owners." I tell him about looking for the camposanto and finding the lone marker. "Yes," he says. "My father told me it was wiped out by a flood. None of the Gonzales is buried in Los Fuertes. They're all buried in the camposanto of San Augustín, or farther downstream at the one in La Concepción."

I have one more question: the church. "Where was it located?" I ask.

"In the ruins you were standing in just before you started back," he says.

Miguel and I look back. Yes, of course. It is not a residence. The windows are set too high. The structure is institutional, not domestic. It has a front entrance and a side entrance. The building is aligned along a northwest-southeast axis, to take advantage of the light.

I am moved to return to what is left of the sanctuary, but we have two other stops to make before the long drive back to Albuquerque—the structure that served as the Presbyterian mission church in Old Town Las Vegas for almost a century, and the cemetery where some of Papá Albino's progeny are buried. I know I must return to Los Fuertes soon. With fresh-cut flowers to place at the solitary grave marker and hardy iris bulbs to plant inside the church ruins. Their yearly appearance will mark the beginning of the growing season.

It has dawned on me that there may be no *campohereje* here. My *protestante* forebears left shortly after they converted and moved upstream to Las Vegas or downstream to La Trementina. Whatever Madrid remains are deposited on the floodplain of Los Fuertes quite likely lie in a consecrated Catholic burial ground. The true *campohereje*, the *protestante* cemetery, is in fact at the foot of the Sangre de Cristo range, in Old Town Las Vegas, not far from the Presbyterian mission church my great-grandfather Albino joined in December 1888.

Miguel and I take our leave of Bernardo and make our way out of the canyon in silence. At the lookout point halfway up, we stop to look down on Los Fuertes. We scan the valley floor for the remains of the camposanto in vain. The shadow of the mesa has extended across the floodplain and creeps slowly up toward the ruins.

At the summit we stop again to look down on San Augustín, already partially in the shade. But farther down the valley the southernmost fields and the west-facing sandstone cliffs are still enjoying the late summer light. The air is becalmed, and a natural silence prevails—no motors, no birdcalls, no cicadas—as if time were suspended. I can smell the resin oozing from the piñon cones, which will soon begin to open, and the pungent odor of ripening juniper berries. A locomotive whistle and the low rumble of railroad cars break the spell. We listen until it is quiet again, then continue our journey into the past.

DOS CAMPOS

† † † Wind sweeps across the *protestante* burial ground, situated on a slope overlooking the Gallinas River Valley, and flattens the tall grass growing within the woven-wire enclosure. The Catholic burial ground, announced by a lofty metal sign over the entrance, flanks it on two sides. The Catholic cemetery is full of gravestones large and small. A number are recent, and all are decorated as if in perpetual commemoration of Memorial Day. The offerings are abundant: plastic bouquets, wreaths, metal crucifixes, Styrofoam crosses, plaster images of saints, and varied representations of the ubiquitous Virgin of Guadalupe.

The Protestant side, however, is somber and lonely. A solitary lilac bush has outgrown a gravesite and obscures the gravestone. An animal path cuts across its northern boundary. My footsteps are the only other thing that has disturbed its dry prairie grass in months. I count the visible grave markers: fewer than twenty. Some are the simple white marble gravestones provided to deceased military veterans. Two of them, set up against the wire fencing that separates

the two cemeteries, mark the burial place of my father's older siblings, José and Elí. Next to them are two granite headstones, one commemorating my grandmother Angelina Gallegos (1885–1958), the other my grandfather Teófilo Madrid (1872–1935). Pushing aside the stiff prairie grass, I find two other tombstones, cast in concrete and sinking into the soil. Here lie Micaela and Susana Madrid, Teófilo's sisters. I look in vain for Papá Albino's grave marker. The remaining tombstones bear familiar *protestante* patronyms: Gallegos, Ordóñez, Lucero, Larrañaga. There are no recent graves.

I stand there in the quiet of the late afternoon with my back to the setting sun. A wind comes up from the east, with a dry, piercing quality that prickles my arms. Like my father before me, I dislike the wind. In the distance I hear a train whistle, elongated as it goes through multiple unprotected crossings. The pitch rises and falls, almost an ululation, then subsides, to be replaced by the muffled sound of the wheels. The rumbling continues until the train passes through the gap at Romeroville.

Miguel continues to take pictures, but my mind and eyes are trained south and east, downstream toward Los Valles and the llano beyond. The canyon the river has cut into the Las Vegas plateau stands in relief, as if marking the way upstream to the bifurcated communities of Old and New Town Las Vegas. The prairie, still in full sunlight, extends north and east from the Sangre de Cristo piedmont and into the horizon, as empty and vast as when my ancestors first ventured into Las Vegas Grandes.

ALBINO MADRID

My great-grandfather, Albino Madrid, was born in 1837, during the brief period when New Mexico was part of the newly established nation of Mexico. He lived seventy-five of his eighty-seven years as a U.S. citizen. His life spans the consolidation of the United States as a continental entity, the violent schism that divided it, and its emergence as a world imperial power. He was born during the exploration and settlement of the Louisiana Purchase, experienced the occupation and lived through the colonization of the Greater Southwest both before and after the Civil War, and witnessed the establishment of the American Empire. Though he lived within a fifty-mile radius, the space he occupied was a microcosm of a larger reality, and the conflicts that raged in the larger national and international arena, including the Civil War, the Spanish-American War, and World War I, played themselves out in his community on a smaller yet no less intense scale.

Albino Madrid is the first of my ancestors to enter modern history. What does that mean, for an individual to enter history? At a micro level, it means becoming widely famous (or infamous) as a consequence of one's deeds. It involves leaving a record of one's life on earth and affecting the course of human events, becoming part of a historical record. Some persons enter history consciously, pursue that end explicitly. Most, however, do so accidentally. They fall into the cauldron of history, so to speak. In some cases the record of the larger collectivity is substantive and historically transcendent, deemed worthy, for better or for worse, of wide public remembrance; in others the mark individuals or a group leave on history is slight and fleeting, of interest only to a subset of the population but of significance to understanding a larger historical experience.

Albino's family does not figure in the records of the Los Valles incident, nor is there any familial memory of Madrid military service in the Civil War, despite the facts that he and two of his siblings are listed in the Territorial Censuses of 1870 and 1880 as being Civil War veterans, and that one of the two New Mexico Civil War battles took place within thirty miles of Los Valles. The heirs of the Las Vegas Land Grant entered history significantly, if unsuccessfully, as participants in the legal challenges to the expropriation of their lands, as well as in the extralegal resistance activities—fence cutting and barn burning—carried out by a group known as Las Gorras Blancas (the White Caps) when their petitions went unanswered or were summarily dismissed. But my

Madrid ancestors do not figure in the records of those activities either, and there is no family memory regarding any engagement in that struggle.

My great-grandfather, however, figured in a historical movement. Toward the end of the nineteenth century, Albino Madrid broke with his historical community and became a *protestante.* When Papá Albino joined the Presbyterian Church in 1888, he became part of the country's historical record. His conversion is recorded in the memoirs of the early Presbyterian missionaries.

In his memoir *Hand on My Shoulder*, Gabino Rendón, a renowned turn-of-the-century Hispano Presbyterian missionary, writes that in the late 1880s he traveled down the Gallinas River from Las Vegas to Los Valles de San Augustín to proselytize but got cold feet and left without speaking with anyone. On his way out of the valley, Don Gabino dropped some biblical tracts by the side of a house. By chance, the house was Albino Madrid's. Shortly thereafter, according to the records of the Presbyterian Church, Papá Albino was received into its fellowship.

Why was he literate? This is what my Anglo and presumably Protestant colleagues who have heard Albino Madrid's story ask. My Hispano Catholic friends, however, want to know why he became an apostate. These questions are the stuff of history, are at the core of imagining who belongs and who does not. They speak deeply to issues of identity.

I have answers, considered ones, but they are not necessarily convincing to my interrogators.

Albino Madrid's literacy is a rather simple matter, complicated only by the historically perverse imagining of the Spanish-Mexican colonizers and their descendants as universally illiterate, ignorant, and resistant to learning. While hardly widespread, much less universal, literacy manifested itself across class and caste.

Literacy was of major concern to both civil and religious authorities during the period when New Mexico was part of the Spanish Empire. Central to the curriculum of schools set up for the Spanish-Mexican settlers was religious doctrine. Pueblo children were enrolled in order to assure their incorporation into Hispano society, particularly after the successful revolt of the Pueblo nations in 1680. The clergy imparted literacy to youthful members of the indigenous population whom they enlisted in their proselytizing efforts. The Spanish colonial world was, furthermore, driven and held together by records, and record keeping demanded a literate class. Members of the officer class had to be literate, and their offspring were the beneficiaries of state-sponsored schooling. Roque Madrid was a *maestro de campo*, a field marshal, and his male offspring and even grandsons would have thus been schooled. Literacy was part of the family's legacy.

Protestant missionaries remember Albino Madrid as the "Bible-reading blacksmith," which the territorial censuses confirm. Tradesmen were historically required to be literate, even at the periphery of the Spanish empire. A condition of serving as an apprentice to a tradesman (including blacksmiths)

was literacy. Prior to moving to the eastern edge of the province in the 1830s, Rafael and his son José Antonio were residents of Santa Fe, the seat of colonial government. Both would have been subject to the conditions of apprenticeship. Even if Albino did not undergo a formal apprenticeship, he probably would have followed that trajectory and become literate.

Significantly, Papá Albino owned an *abecedario*, the most fundamental instrument for literacy. It is not likely that he was the first of his family to hold it. Certainly, as the census and church records suggest, it contributed to the literacy of his extended family. It would have been a precious possession, yet he traded it for a Bible.

What was lacking in the New Mexican colonial world, which Diego de Vargas, the warrior-ruler who retook the province of New Mexico after the Pueblo Revolt, termed "remote beyond compare," were materials to read. Historians document the colony's paucity of books, as well as the caution exercised by owners of books, given the presence of the Office of the Inquisition.

Schooling increasingly became a state concern after secularization in the 1820s. Mexico's successful struggle for independence from Spain, moreover, provided a political environment conducive to education, literacy, the publication and circulation of printed materials, and political liberalism. Native cleric Antonio Martínez of Taos, the primary intellectual Hispano of the period, sought to advance both through his printing press, newspaper, and college. As a central part of his efforts to provide his community with the intellectual wherewithal to defend themselves against changes in their world, Padre Martínez utilized the press he helped bring from Chihuahua to print and circulate spelling books and other materials to foment literacy.

That state of affairs would change radically, of course, with the U.S. occupation and its imposition of English as the language of government and its agencies, and subsequently with the American Catholic Church's takeover of the recently secularized Mexican Catholic Church. Unlike the trappers and traders who preceded them, the new lords of the land were Protestants. Public education, were it to be provided, would be in English, not the language of the conquered. The French-born, French-speaking Archbishop Lamy, sent from Ohio to New Mexico to counter Anglo Protestants' proselytizing activities, resisted the introduction of public education, informed as it was by Protestantism and liberalism. In so doing, he also blocked the liberalizing efforts of Padre Martínez, who was desperately trying to create a space between the Anglo-Protestant and Anglo-Catholic hegemonies. Literacy rates dropped in the first two decades of the occupation and rose only as Hispanos rallied to protect themselves from the depredations of the new society. The principal instruments became Spanish-language newspapers, which flourished in the last decades of the nineteenth century, as A. Gabriel Melendez has so eloquently documented in *So All Is Not Lost.*

The first books available to the populace were written in English. Religious tracts were the exception, in particular those used by Protestant missionaries in their proselytizing activities, such as the Bible. Spanish-language Bibles made their way down the Santa Fe Trail in the decade following New Mexico's occupation. The American Bible Society republished the Valera translation in 1865, with an eye to missionary activity in the New Mexico Territory and Latin America. Albino Madrid exchanged his spelling book, quite likely one produced by Padre Martínez, for one of these Bibles and then proceeded to read and share it with family and friends. It was not until the end of the century, when the railways extending north from Mexico connected with the east-west railways of the United States, that books from Spain and the Americas became generally available to the Spanish-speaking inhabitants of Greater Mexico.

What, then, led Albino and his brothers Pablo and Antonio to become Protestants? Religious conversion in the Americas, Ramón Gutiérrez, the distinguished historian of New Mexico, tells me, has three historical explanations: coercion, seduction, or advantage. But they do not seem to apply to the *protestantes* of New Mexico. Coercion involves force, and the violence Albino Madrid and his parents undoubtedly experienced firsthand in the military attack on their village in 1847 in combination with the expropriation of their land holdings toward the end of the century would have made them resistant to coercion.

To be sure, the attractions of the new society—material goods, education, economic opportunity—could be construed as seduction. The villagers were undoubtedly captivated by the technology—trains, presses, pumps—introduced into their midst. But the availability of material goods was not

matched by a corresponding increase in the wherewithal to purchase them. Most Hispanos remained tied to a barter economy and entered the cash economy slowly and late. Economic opportunity was more apparent than real. Hispano merchants and entrepreneurs found themselves at a disadvantage in an English-speaking world and its networks. Hispano workers ended up in a two-tier labor structure, and the cost of living frequently exceeded their wages.

There was some social advantage to conversion: access to education and to health care. But the elementary schools and clinics the Presbyterian missionaries established throughout the villages of the Rio Arriba, as well as the boarding schools Allison-James (for girls) in Santa Fe and Menaul (for boys) in Albuquerque, were available to Protestants and Catholics alike.

Papá Albino's knowledge of the Old Testament, as conveyed to me by my father; the fact that Madrid is a surname common to fifteenth- and sixteenth-century Jewish converts to Catholicism; and my historical ignorance led me early on to speculate that Albino might have been a crypto-Jew whose religious background and inclinations were nurtured when he came in contact with Protestant missionaries. This school of thought has numerous adherents in New Mexico, including the descendants of the early *protestantes*. The evidence and arguments for a significant Hispano Jewish heritage as advanced by its advocates, however, appears strained to me. I have found no textual evidence to support such speculation in the case of Albino Madrid.

I believe Papá Albino's conversion was a logical outcome of being literate and resulted from the epiphany he experienced upon reading the Bible. But the conditions of the period provide a compelling historical context. These included the experience of the Catholic faithful outside the principal population centers; the role and experience of the Penitente Brotherhood, a lay society that acted in place of an absent laity and subsequently in defiance of the official church; Archbishop Lamy's rejection of the Mexican Catholic practices and clergy; and Padre Martínez and his followers' struggle to carve out a Hispano cultural, political, and religious space in a changed environment.

The Catholic community that lived outside of Santa Fe, Santa Cruz, Taos, and Las Vegas did not have the ready services of the clergy at hand for a good part of the century. In their absence, parishioners fell back on their lay societies to sustain them spiritually, most notably the Third Order of Saint Francis, best known as the Penitente Brotherhood. Lamy's attempts to stamp out their practices alienated the faithful in those parishes. The Penitentes persisted in them, thereby affirming their cultural heritage, notwithstanding the condemnations of Catholic prelates or Protestant missionaries. Lamy's campaign against Padre Martínez and the native clergy he had been nurturing at his college in Taos resulted in an oppositional faction among Martínez's supporters. Protestantism provided an alternative to those who rejected the Penitentes' practices and the American Catholic Church's policies as introduced by Lamy. Among them were Martínez's relations and friends, who subsequently formed a Presbyterian congregation in Taos.

What is there to understand? my informants, the *protestante* relatives, friends, and acquaintances I have interrogated over the years, ask in bafflement. To them, the answer is clear. Direct access to the Gospel, to the Word of God, to the Truth as revealed by the Bible led their parents and grandparents to the church. Some, to be sure, recount stories of conflict with clergy that led to their ancestors' break with Catholicism; others speak of the blandishments offered by missions, namely health care and education; still others tell of personal aid provided by the Protestant missionaries. But all accept and affirm the self-evident nature of conversion. It was God's will and God's plan.

††† *Con el alambre vino el hambre* was a refrain I often heard the elders voice. Barbed wire and hunger arrived hand in hand. In fact, it could be said that both arrived by rail. The railroad linking Las Vegas with the eastern half of the continent transformed my Hispano ancestors' world. It made possible the rapid growth of the Anglo-American population and fueled economic development, which exacerbated tensions between Hispanos and Anglos, Catholics and Protestants, Democrats and Republicans, ranchers and farmers, landholding *patrones* and landless *paisanos*. The Anglo-American population also brought with them a new political and legal system that had profound and negative implications for the Hispano way of life.

By the end of the nineteenth century, land speculators had driven the majority of the villagers of Los Valles de San Augustín from their communal holdings. Most of the residents abandoned the valley sometime between 1890 and 1910. The immediate cause was loss of access to the common lands of their former land grant, fenced off by new owners after the U.S. Court of Land Claims rejected the claims of the original settlers and their heirs to the land they held in common and which they depended on for their existence.

Residents could no longer pasture their flocks on *las vegas grandes*, gather firewood in *el monte*, or cut timber in the sierra. In addition, their yields of corn, squash, legumes, melons, and fruit—subsistence level at best given the limited amount of arable land—declined sharply as the waters of the Gallinas River were diverted for use upstream and became increasingly polluted.

Most of the residents went downstream and then south and east into the llano as far as Kansas, Oklahoma, and the Texas Panhandle in search of pasture for their flocks. At some point in the 1890s Albino's younger brothers also moved downstream to homestead the northwestern edge of the Llano Estacado and to build what became known in time as the *protestante* community of La Trementina.

At a moment when his neighbors and kinfolk were moving downstream to preserve their traditional way of life, my great-grandfather Albino Madrid, his brother Pablo, and their respective progeny moved upriver, toward the future, to the commercial and cultural center of Las Vegas. In addition to being pushed out of Los Valles, they were pulled by their connection with fellow Protestants in Las Vegas and the new society's educational and economic opportunities. The families settled on the western bank of the Gallinas River, near the plaza of what became known as Old Town, to distinguish it from New Town, the Anglo community formed on the eastern bank along the tracks of the newly arrived Atchison, Topeka & Santa Fe Railroad in 1879.

I have often asked myself whether Albino Madrid and his *protestante* kin conceived their departure as a metaphorical banishment from Eden or as a deliverance from Egypt, a figurative journey to the Promised Land. Albino and his fellow residents were dispossessed by persons who manipulated the new economic, legal, and political system and sought to keep the Hispano population tied to the old one. In moving upstream, my great-grandfather may have been of the opinion that the new order might afford him and his family economic opportunity, social advancement, and protection under the law. The railroad whistle they heard upstream would have constituted a siren's song calling them to modernity. I believe Papá Albino and his family actively sought to become part of the new society, a society he undoubtedly perceived to be not only dynamic but also perhaps democratic and just. Most important, he would integrate his family into his new community of faith.

Papá Albino lived out the last two decades of his life—a life that spanned two centuries, two economies, three governments, and two cultures—in Las Vegas. The censuses of 1900, 1910, and 1920 list his occupation alternatively as blacksmith and silversmith. He lived on Socorro Street, owned his home, and is recorded as being literate. He rejoined the church whose fellowship he was first admitted to in 1888: the Spanish Presbyterian mission church of Las Vegas, established in 1884 and abandoned in 1960 but still located on an east-facing slope overlooking the vast meadows from which Las Vegas took its name.

Los Valles de San Augustín continues to exert the same pull on me that it did on my father. I have returned to the valley many times since I first visited it in my father's company over two decades ago. It is seasonally populated. Once the harvest season is over, most families move to Las Vegas, since few vehicles can navigate the dirt road leading out of the canyon once the rains start. Only a few hardy souls brave the winter there.

The valley changes character with the seasons. Seen from the lip of the canyon, in winter it is sere and lonely. Its most prominent features are the narrow long-lot fields bisecting the valley and the sandstone cliffs on either side. The landscape brightens in the spring as the ground cover comes back to life and blossoms grace the gnarled fruit trees. The Gallinas River, usually a series of small pools, overflows its banks and deposits sienna-colored silt on the

floodplain. Summer's plentitude manifests itself in the lush growth along the acequia, in the meadows' swaying grass, in the rustling leaves of the ancient cottonwoods. Late summer is marked by the sounds of mowing and baling machines. Viewed from the lip of the canyon, the hay bales scattered on the meadows resemble pieces in a board game.

My favorite time of year is early autumn, when the vegetation reflects the delicate palette of the canyon walls and the Gallinas is flowing full and clear, its waters no longer diverted for irrigation. School has commenced, and the families have left. A goat leads a small herd down the bluff, and the plaintive wail of a locomotive whistle echoes off the canyon walls. On my visits, I sometimes encounter local residents. They are guarded until I establish my bona fides, then move on to leave me to my reverie.

THE INTERLOPER

† † † "This is not Mills." My father's voice is swept away by the wind coursing through the grass and along the gravel road. He is so slight that the wind almost bends him. The only other sound in the emptiness that surrounds us is the whirring of cicadas. Before us stands a shed with a sign. My son, Raúl, reads it aloud: "P.O. Mills NM 87302 Hours: 1:00–1:30 M–F." There is nothing else. Beyond the shed, to the east, lie grasslands; to the north, grasslands; to the south, more grasslands. Behind us, to the west, is a slight rise. We are at the western edge of the Kiowa National Grasslands, located in northeastern New Mexico and established in the middle of the Depression.

I have been hearing the name Mills for almost half a century. My father taught school there before he married my mother and moved to Rio Arriba County. The family album includes photos from that period of his life. They show a dapper, exceptionally handsome young man posing with the Mills High School men's and women's basketball teams. He is not much older than they are, but they are all larger than he is. Mills has been part of my father's memories, and he has imprinted it in the minds of his children and grandchildren as well.

My father traveled to Mills for the first time in the summer of 1935. He was twenty-four years old and looking for a teaching position. One was not available to him in his hometown. In West Las Vegas he was a *protestante*; in East Las Vegas he was a Mexican. My father and a friend drove north and east in a borrowed automobile to the Anglo farming and ranching communities of Mora, Harding, and Colfax counties. In each community they sought out the chairman of the local school board. By prior agreement they spoke for each other: "Mr. Miller, I'd like you to meet my colleague, Arthur T. Madrid, a senior at New Mexico Highlands University. He is seeking a teaching position. His majors are English and business education, but he can also teach Spanish." The interview concluded, they moved on to the next settlement.

Chance gave my father a teaching position at Mills. The two Anglo school board members each had a candidate and could reach no agreement or accommodation on them. In the end they turned to the third member of the board, whose name coincidentally was Madrid, and asked him to choose. He chose the Mexican.

My father stands before the erstwhile post office, perplexed. It is a hot, dry August afternoon. He turns left and then right. He looks north, then south, west, east. He shakes his head. There is just a sea of grass and the skeleton of a town: three long-abandoned dwellings and a cement grain tower that rises out of the prairie.

We climb back into the car and take a gravel road to the top of the rise. In the distance lies the canyon cut into the high prairie by the Canadian River and its tributaries. Ranch buildings stand along the road leading west. To the north we can see a ranch house but no sign of human life.

My father's puzzlement and the afternoon heat overcome my usual temer-

ity. I do not go gently into rural, western, Anglo space. It is a function of both acquired and transmitted wisdom, reinforced when we drive up to the ranch house and are met by two large dogs.

A woman, large and raw-boned, appears and calls to them. From the safety of the car, I explain: "Sorry to trouble you. We're looking for Mills. My father was a schoolteacher there, in the 1930s. We found the post office but nothing else. Could you direct us?" She is hatless and sleeveless, and her exposed skin is a prickly red. Her face registers surprise and curiosity. "Taught here, you say?" I nod. "In the 1930s?" I nod again. "What was his name?" I tell her. "Taught business education?" she asks. "Yes," I answer, nodding vigorously.

She invites us in. The dogs follow at a distance. It is a modest house. We enter the living room tentatively. Afternoon heat and summer dust hang in the air.

"Sam, we have visitors," she calls out as she disappears into the back of the house. A bulky, elderly man appears from an adjacent room. He is wearing rumpled overalls and a faded work shirt. He has been napping. His hair is matted, his eyes swollen. The skin below his hairline is a ruddy red.

The woman returns with a pitcher of ice water and glasses. "Man says he was a schoolteacher here in the 1930s," she tells him. "Says he taught business education."

He greets us and invites us to sit. "From Las Vegas?" he asks.

"Yes," my father replies.

"I remember you," he says.

We sit down, surprised.

"They're looking for Mills," she says. Her voice is loud, to compensate for his hearing, she tells us.

"Nothing left anymore," he says, matter-of-factly. "We're about the only old-timers here. Most people left during the Depression, when the federal government bought the land around here for the grasslands park. Only a few of us stayed. Our children grew up and left." He says it dispassionately. There is no note of loss or regret.

"I'm one of the Johnson girls," the woman tells my father. "I had already graduated, but when I found out you taught business education I came back for a year."

My father nods and says, "Yes, yes."

We drink the ice water. In the background I can hear the whirring of a windmill. My father, to my surprise, asks very few questions. Our visit is marked principally by silence. After a polite interval, we take our leave.

MY FATHER arrived in Mills on a hot early September afternoon in 1935. To get there he took an Atchison, Topeka & Santa Fe train northeast from Las Vegas to French, where he spent the night. The next day he rode the caboose of a Southern Pacific ore train southeast to Mills. He took a room at the Libert Hotel for a dollar a day, meals included. After a week he became a boarder at a

private residence. For the next two years he taught school at Mills, and during the summers he completed the requirements for his baccalaureate degree.

We get back in the car and return to the shed. As we walk south down the gravel road my father stops. “I see it now,” he says. “The houses were all in a row along the road, facing east. On the opposite side were the general store, the post office, the blacksmith shop, and the garage. Over there was the Libert Hotel.”

There is no sign of their existence, not even foundation stone. He stands in the middle of the road for a long time. Mills is a graveyard of memories for him. The wind weaves through the tall grass. We walk slowly up the lane to the car, pausing as my father recalls where a building stood or a family lived. A powdery dust covers our shoes. Ever fastidious, he brushes it off before getting into the car.

The sun is low on the horizon, and the wind has risen. My father is quiet as we head north toward Springer and the interstate that will take us back to Las

Vegas. "That first morning," he says, finally, "when I walked down the road to the schoolhouse, everybody came out on their front porches to see the Mexican schoolteacher. I remember I wore a black hat, and they pointed at me. They continued to do so all fall, until the cold drove them in.

"They didn't want me in their community," he continues. "The boys would harass me constantly in and out of class. The worst was a teacher, Miss Jones, who ragged me unmercifully. Every night I would return to my room and pack my suitcase. And every night my landlady would say to me, 'Don't do it, Mr. Madrid. Don't leave. Don't you see that's what they want you to do?'

"I went home that first Thanksgiving," he says. "After church on Sunday I took a bus to Springer and caught a ride east to the Mills junction. It was late afternoon by then. I started walking south toward Mills, sixteen miles away. The afternoon was cold, and as the sun dropped it got colder. There were no cars on the road. One came by after I had walked halfway to Mills. It slowed down, then sped off. I recognized the family. At dusk I left the highway and walked to a ranch house I saw in the distance. I offered to pay them to drive me the rest of the way."

Raúl asks my father why he returned the next year. He laughs and says, "Nothing had changed. I needed a job, and the one at Mills was the only one available." When we turn south onto the interstate, the sun is dropping behind the Sangre de Cristo range and the prairie to the east is luminous. He gazes into the distance. Finally he says, "Sam, the man we met, was one of the worst. He had already graduated but showed up with his brothers for every school function. They were particularly unpleasant at basketball games."

Two weeks into his third year, my father was offered a position in Luna County at a higher salary. He packed his bag that night and left the next morning without collecting the pay due him. Although he knocked the dust off his shoes as he departed, Mills is deeply engraved in his memory, and the lines are etched as sharp as ever.

THE CHOSEN PEOPLE

† † † When Albino Madrid and his family moved to Las Vegas sometime during the 1890s to become part of the new society and integrate themselves into their new religious community, Anglo Americans had already established a community on the east bank of the Gallinas River, leaving their Hispano brothers and sisters in Christ behind in what was a hostile social and political space.

In the United States, and in particular in the West, railroad tracks have historically been the dividing line between communities. The railroad created the physical split between the two communities of Las Vegas, but the Gallinas River reinforced the divide. As the nineteenth century came to an end, the river that had originally provided sustenance and community to Albino and his neighbors ceased to do so, yet it continued to play a significant role in their lives.

Like the Israelites and the early Christians, the Hispano Protestants felt chosen by God, and like them they found themselves besieged. In parallel fashion to the *fuertes*, the fortifications Hispano settlers built on the frontier to protect themselves against indigenous marauders, the Hispano converts to Protestantism had to erect psychological barriers to protect themselves from the hostility of their former Catholic coreligionists, who now called them *herejes* and worse. They came to see themselves as superior in their thinking, values, and behavior to their Hispano Catholic neighbors and relations, and they used those attitudes to shield themselves against religious antagonism.

Hispano Protestants found themselves in separate congregations from their Anglo brothers and sisters in Christ. Despite their accommodations—speaking English, becoming educated, taking on the values and ways of their Anglo brethren—Hispano Protestants would continue to be perceived by members of the new society as being different in degree but not in kind from their Catholic kin. They became unwitting beneficiaries of the legacy of

Anglo-American racial ideology, which saw them as mixed-bloods, biologically and socially inferior, therefore less capable, and thus unworthy. As such, they found themselves between two worlds: one that was hostile to them because they were apostates and another that kept them at arm's length because they were manifestly the "other." Disdained by their mentors, the Hispano Protestants nonetheless reaffirmed their faith in the new society and its values. Fortified by their beliefs, they raised high their defenses against Catholic hostility and Anglo rejection and began forging space for themselves in Anglo-American society and its institutions.

In becoming a Protestant, Albino Madrid participated in the splitting of what had by and large been a homogeneous community of Hispanos. Theirs must have been a trying existence, suspended as they were between their historical community—one that included relatives—and their newfound community of faith, which, although it included family and friends, was inextricably tied to the new society. Aggressive Protestant missionary activity, in keeping with the virulently anti-Catholic character of nineteenth-century American Protestantism, made the split even more visible. One unpleasant public event illustrates the awkward situation Hispano Protestants found themselves in.

In 1901, in Las Vegas, a *junta de indignación* took place, a public rally called by Hispano leaders to protest a newspaper article published by a Presbyterian missionary. Although no copy of the article survives, according to Phillip Gonzales in *Forced Sacrifice as Ethnic Protest*, newspaper

reports indicate that Ms. Nellie Snyder, the author of the article, "disparaged Hispanos' customs, the state of their homes, their cooking, and, most notably, their mixed racial inheritance." Although the larger context for the gathering was one of cultural antagonism, religious antipathy, and political conflict, what principally informed Hispano political leaders' reaction to her article was her characterization of the Hispano population's biological makeup, and what was recorded was their outrage at being constructed as *mestizos*.

The only photograph that exists of Albino Madrid was most likely taken in 1921, a year before his death. He is seated on a chair outdoors, in front of the doorway to the *fuerte*, a log structure that stood next to the *fragua*, his blacksmith's forge. A small child, my aunt Myrtle, who was born in the summer of 1920, sits on his lap and waves what appears to be a flower. She is fair-skinned, and her hair is fine and light-colored. To her right stands my uncle Tito, who would have been five years old. Tito is wearing bib overalls and a white shirt. He is looking down, his face in shadow. The only visible part of his head is his hair, which is very fine and straight, unlike the curly matted hair of his mature years. My father stands behind him, staring directly at the camera as was his wont. Only his head is visible. He shares his brother's fine, straight dark hair. His eyes already have the mournful look that marked him and his siblings.

Papá Albino is wearing a three-piece suit. His shirt, dark and striped, is buttoned at the collar. A watch chain hangs from his vest. In his jacket pocket are a tobacco pouch and pipe. His dark skin is accentuated by his white beard and hair, which is thick and curly. His features are clearly African.

Friends, on seeing the portrait, comment on his skin color and indigenous features. These I take for granted. We are *mestizos*. The founding colonizers included few women, and most were *mestizas*. Unions with Pueblo women, forced and unforced, furthered *mestizaje*. Virtually every Hispano has *genízaros*, whether of Apache, Comanche, Navajo, or Ute origin, in the family line. Our *mestizo* complexions and features, moreover, precede even those that

stem from our indigenous heritage, whether Mexican or New Mexican. We are the product of the mixtures of Mediterranean, North African, and Southern European populations. Lacking any context, however, Albino's portrait could easily be mistaken for that of an aged African American posing in the garden with the master's children. A striking photographic portrait of my grandmother Angelina Gallegos Madrid, my aunt Myrtle, and my uncle Rolando that hung in the dining room of the Madrid home in Las Vegas speaks to the range of phenotypes in Hispano families. It is an iconic image, reflecting the seventeenth- and eighteenth-century figurative representations of Europe, Africa, and the Americas as females—one black, one white, one brown. Grandmother Angelina is dark, and she could have fit easily into any Hispano or Puebloan family; Rolando's skin coloring, tight curly hair, and pronounced lips would have permitted him to meld into an African American community; Myrtle is light-skinned, indistinguishable in her features, manner, or style from the American women of the period.

Given the fundamentally religious nature of his affiliation with Presbyterians, Albino Madrid would undoubtedly have sympathized with their antipathy toward Catholicism. To be a Presbyterian was to be one of God's chosen, and he would have inevitably also taken on his fellow Protestants' social and cultural values, including their intense pietism and their characterization of the Hispano Catholic population as benighted and backward. Certainly he and his fellow Hispano *protestantes* would have sought to emulate the ways of their Anglo Protestant brethren and would have disdained those of their Hispano Catholic neighbors.

I wonder how Albino Madrid, given his evident racial makeup, felt about the Hispano population's racialization by a coreligionist, and particularly by a missionary he would have been in close contact with. An avid reader, he would have been very aware of Anglo racial attitudes. In theory, he could have rationalized Anglo bigotry as a function of religious antipathy, but in becoming a Protestant he had become one of "them." Yet here was no run-of-the-mill Anglo, not simply a fellow Protestant but a Presbyterian missionary, relegating him to permanent lesser status.

I have remained curious about the incident. The Hispano Protestants were brave folk who risked familial and social opprobrium for their beliefs. According to my father, Papá Albino enjoyed arguing in public about religion, and I cannot help but believe that Albino Madrid spoke up in defense of Nellie Snyder in 1901.

MYRTLE, MERTOLA, LALA

† † † Lala called twice while I was out. Even though we speak on the telephone only occasionally, and despite the distortions of my answering machine, it is unmistakably her voice, singular and familiar, made more plaintive than usual by worry. "How are you, *mijito*? Take care of yourself. You are my rock."

She is my father's sister. The only girl, the youngest child. My favorite aunt, my main connection to my father's family, the last remaining fund of familial memory. Myrtle to the world. *Mertola en familia y en español.* Lala—a child's name—to me and then to her siblings and subsequently to mine.

I return her call. "Hello," she answers. It is more a question than a statement. Not the bright, cheery greeting I remember.

I reassure her that I am well. That I'm home and healthy, that the procedure went smoothly. Like my father, like me, she does not linger on the phone. She uses it to touch base, and once she has made contact she is satisfied. I try to sustain the connection, to compensate for my sporadic attention to her, for my few calls and even fewer visits. She responds laconically to my questions. Everything is fine. Daughter Lauri is looking forward to vacation break. Brother Rolo is still acting as if he's at ringside while he watches wrestling matches on TV. It's cold. It's windy. It's hot. It hasn't rained. Las Vegas hasn't changed. Nothing going on. I tell her I will visit her at the end of the summer. She still remembers some familial stories, though she says she doesn't. They come hard. There is too much pain in many of the memories.

On one of my visits Lala gave me a sketch of her father, Teófilo Madrid, along with a copy of his certificate of graduation from the Southwest School of Theology. There seems to be little by way of family documents or mementos, and she is not one to part what remains of them. "You should have this," she said. "You are the keeper of the memories."

I recognize the sketch, taken from a formal photograph I have seen in a history of Presbyterian missionary activity in New Mexico. The man in the photograph and sketch and the man in family snapshots bear little resemblance to each other. The Teófilo Madrid of the portrait is slim, with a full head of hair and an elegant mustache. His posture is stiff, and his eyes signal determination. The Teófilo of the family snapshots, dressed in work clothes, clean-shaven and relaxed, is a dark-skinned man with a receding hairline. There is a bemused half-smile on his face, but the mournful eyes of his children are evident in his own.

My paternal grandfather, Teófilo Madrid, died four years before I was born. By the time I could formulate other than superficial questions about him, the family memory had dimmed. Dad held him in great respect and described him as tight-lipped, stern, and impatient. Only Lala spoke of him with affection. Barely fourteen years old when he passed away, she has just two recollections of her father. In one she is at a carnival with him in the evening, captivated by what is going on around her. She takes what she assumes is her father's hand, only to look up and see her father standing at a distance, smiling at her in sweet amusement. In the second she is at home reading to her mother in Spanish from a hymnal. She looks up and sees her father, who has also been reading, nodding at her mother and beaming with pride.

Teófilo Madrid was fifty-one when Lala was born. The New Mexico Territorial Census of 1900 lists his profession as schoolteacher. He is married to Sofia, and they have a six-month-old son, Eliceo Alfredo. Both are recorded as literate and as speaking English.

"He smoked a pipe," Lala tells me after Sunday dinner as I query her in an effort to learn more about her parents. "He used to say, '*Qué* fine *pipa*.' " She giggles.

Intrigued by the odd mixture of English and Spanish, I say, "Didn't he speak English?"

"Yes, he did," she says, in the deliberate and precise way of speaking characteristic of my father and his siblings. Then she adds, "But not as well as Mother did. And he had a marked accent. He read the *Optic*, our local newspaper, to us aloud after dinner."

Teófilo Madrid enrolled in the Southwest School of Theology, a school for Hispano evangelists set up in conjunction with a Presbyterian college in Del Norte, Colorado, midway through the 1890s. He was in the second cohort

of Hispanos matriculated at the seminary. The photographic portrait of the school's second graduating class, dated 1899, reveals him to be in good company. Among his fellow graduates, all pioneer Hispano Presbyterian evangelists, were his older cousin, Manuel Madrid, as well as the legendary Gabino Rendón, the timid missionary responsible for Papá Albino's conversion.

Unlike most of his classmates, my grandfather never became a pastor of a church. I once asked my father why. As usual he demurred, saying he didn't know, but then he said, "There were probably more *evangelistas* than there were positions in the mission field. And he would not have been welcome at the Anglo churches." The synod could support only a limited number of missionaries, and because they were not ordained ministers the Hispano evangelists could not aspire to being called to lead an Anglo congregation, even if they had mastered English.

Teófilo Madrid became a schoolteacher instead, but never in the schools of Old Town or New Town. In 1909 he was the principal of the public school in La Trementina, a full day's trip by buggy across the vega and down the Canadian Escarpment. Usually his postings were closer to home, in one-room schoolhouses in the little communities in and around Las Vegas. During my father's adolescence, Teófilo made a daily trek by horseback to El Mesteño, a village in the foothills of the sierra west of Las Vegas. Dad was responsible for saddling up the horse, El Bayo, in the morning. Dad's oldest brother, Elí, told of borrowing a Model T Ford to travel to a more distant village, Gabaldón, to fetch his father, who took ill midweek and was unable to ride El Bayo home at week's end.

Late in his life I asked my father why Grandfather Teófilo never held a teaching position in Las Vegas. He remained quiet for a good while and then said, "We were *protestantes*, and thus he couldn't be employed in Old Town. And since we were Mexicans, he couldn't get a job in New Town."

The political history of New Mexico is curious. Like all political histories, it is complicated and contradictory. Its electorate, in addition to being divided along the traditional lines of rich and poor, urban and rural, natives and new arrivals, Anglos and Hispanos, Democrats and Republicans, Secessionists and Unionists, was also split along theological lines: Protestants of various stripes and Catholics. Apart from the Irish Catholics, the Anglo population of New Mexico was overwhelmingly Protestant. The political differences among the Protestant Anglo Americans were great, but they were united by their disdain for Mexicans and Indians and by their even greater dislike of Catholics. Hispanos distrusted their Anglo Catholic brethren but made alliances of convenience with them when necessary.

Close ties between church and state existed in both communities, but where Hispanos dominated, church and state operated hand in hand. This was especially true where schools were concerned. Hispanos preferred parochial schools staffed by nuns and priests to secular public schools, and they underwrote the former with public funds. Anglos promoted public schooling but resisted setting up a public system whenever Hispanos held an electoral majority. In Old Town Las Vegas, Hispano Catholics held sway and only Catholics staffed their schools; in New Town Las Vegas the same was true of Protestants, except that it didn't include Hispano Protestants. Grandfather Teófilo's only option was to teach where others wouldn't—in the rural schools of San Miguel County, located in remote communities that during the winter months were only accessible by horseback.

Teófilo, like his father Albino, experienced firsthand the defining moments of modern U.S. history: the Anglo consolidation of the New Mexico Territory, the Spanish-American War, the drawn-out struggle over statehood, and World War I. An educated man, he would have understood how the new economic, legal, and political system was imposing itself and further marginalizing the Hispano populace. A young adult when the Court of Land Claims ruled definitively against the Hispano land grant heirs, he would have witnessed the anger and frustration of the dispossessed. While he was in evangelical school in Colorado, Theodore Roosevelt was recruiting New Mexicans for the war against Spain. Las Vegas was the prime arena for organizing as Hispanos attempted to advance their political interests, defend their cultural heritage, and improve their socioeconomic status. The acrimonious struggle for New Mexico statehood, which was informed not only by the continuing economic and political tensions between northerners and southerners, but particularly by Anglo-American social and racial ideology, played itself out during his early adulthood. Neither he nor his children were caught up by World War I, but his relatives were. A good many of them also died from the influenza of 1918. Whatever advantage the Madrid family acquired during the boom of the 1920s was lost during the Great Depression.

Teófilo Madrid died in 1935, in the middle of the Depression. He had been unable to secure a teaching appointment since 1932. The family sentiment is that his illness was aggravated, perhaps even caused, by being unemployed.

Republicans held sway in San Miguel County, and family lore has it that the politicos punished him for voting for Franklin Delano Roosevelt in the 1932 presidential election.

I wish Grandfather Teófilo had lived long enough for me to know him. Like him, I prepared for a career as a Presbyterian minister. Like him, I left it behind. Unlike me, he remained engaged with the church and in contact with his fellow evangelists. None of his children felt themselves called to a religious vocation. All except his oldest son remained believers and, to a greater or lesser extent, active members of the church. My sense of him is that he came to terms with his marginal professional and social status but was highly aware of the contradictions and ironies of being a Hispano and a Protestant. I suspect that despite his gruff and laconic nature, he might have been disposed to take up with me the complex situation of being a heretic and an interloper.

ANGELINA GALLEGOS

† † † No family tree recorded in the family Bible, no familial stories passed down over the years, no family history counted and recounted exists for my paternal grandmother, née Angelina Gallegos, whom my siblings and I referred to as Grandma Madrid to distinguish her from our maternal grandmother, Trinidad Tafoya Barela. Whether Angelina chose not to pass on any information about her origins or whether my father and his siblings were not particularly interested in learning much about her family is not clear. Dad thought perhaps she was an orphan, but his brother Tito, always protective of the family, objected strenuously when Dad said so. Dad also speculated that perhaps Mamá Efigenia, an elderly woman who lived with them when he was a child, was related to his mother. Lala reported that Grandma had a brother, José, who died in a mining accident. All the siblings remembered Grandma's cousin, Anastasio Gallegos, known to them as Tío Nasty, and his children Abel,

Rubel, and Hadita. They had all moved to Colorado, where Rubel died from a black widow spider's bite.

What I found compelling is the suggestion that Grandma had broken with her family. My father and his siblings recounted an occasion in which a visitor informed her that he had run into her relatives in town. "*Vi a tus parientes*," the visitor is alleged to have told her. And to a person, all recall that her response was "*No me hables de ellos*." She did not want to hear about them. They never found out who the *parientes* were or why that was the case. Dad thought they might have been relatives who remained Catholics.

They did know that in 1903 she married the widower schoolmaster, Teófilo, thirteen years her senior, following the death of his wife, Sofia, in 1902. How, where, or when Angelina and Teófilo met is not known to the family. She apparently took over the care of his son, Eliceo Alfredo, after Sofia died. An entry in the *Registro de familia* of the Madrid family Bible records that Angelina and Teófilo married in September 1903. She was eighteen years old. In 1906, with the birth of Elí, Angelina became a mother herself. The 1910 census records that they have three children, Alfredo, Elí, and José. My father was born in 1911, Tito in 1913, Rolando (Rolo) in 1917, and Myrtle in 1921.

When Grandmother Angelina passed away in 1958, the memory of the Gallegos family died with her. My initial attempts to track her down in the genealogical materials of the New Mexico State Historical Archives were unsuccessful. For reasons unknown there are no extant copies of the 1890 census, taken five years after the birth date engraved on her tombstone, and she does not figure in the 1900 census.

While exploring the archives of the Menaul Historical Library, I found Angelina Gallegos on the rolls of the Allison-James boarding school, operated by the Presbyterian Church in Santa Fe for many years. She had enrolled there in 1898 and was listed as attending in 1899 and 1900 as well, but she did not return in the fall of 1901. Her hometown is recorded as Chaperito, the last of the Los Valles de San Augustín settlements, located at the mouth of the Gallinas River, ten miles downstream from Los Fuertes, the Madrid family homestead. The register of the Allison-James School also records that she spoke English and that she had been admitted to membership in the Presbyterian Church. She most likely attended the Presbyterian mission school at Chaperito before going to Allison-James, but I was unable to find the records for the school.

Cousin Lorraine Romero Aguilar, the family genealogist, who plows through parish and census records with great determination and ability, was more successful than I was. Grandmother Angelina, she determined, was born to Cesaria Gallegos, daughter of Francisco Gallegos and Efigenia Gutiérrez. Angelina is the product of a union between Cesaria and Encarnación Herrera, who were married in 1879. She was evidently brought up by her grandmother, the Mamá Efigenia who lived and died in the Madrid household, but she retained her mother's patronymic, Gallegos.

Regarding her mother, Cesaria, the historical records are equally scant.

She is listed in the baptismal records as the mother of another daughter, born twelve years earlier, in 1873. The minutes of the Las Vegas Presbyterian Church record that in February 1890 Cesaria joined the congregation formed at Los Valles. Cesaria's father, her brother Francisco, and her cousins Anastasio and Genoveva had presented themselves for acceptance into the church the previous year. Dad's speculation that her estrangement from her relatives might be about religion was thus rendered invalid. Angelina Gallegos remains a cryptic figure. Fiercely loyal to her husband and family, the only Gallegos she maintained a relationship with were her uncle Anastasio and her cousins Abel, Rubel, and Hadita. No one in the family seems to have met her mother, father, sister, or brother.

Grandmother Angelina was less than five feet tall, but she presided over the Madrid household. No one contradicted her, and her offspring did as she said. Whether Grandma became the matriarch when her husband died or was already established as such is not clear to me. Dad referred to her as the disciplinarian of the family, in part I suspect because his father was away so much of the time. But it was Grandma who wrote letters to Dad and his brothers when they were pining away at boarding school in Albuquerque; who would not send Myrtle to boarding school, although she herself had left home at age fourteen to attend the Allison-James School; who secured a personal loan to send Dad across town to study at the university, in the middle of the Depression, while Grandfather Teófilo was still alive.

I believe she would have preferred that all her children remain with her. Leaving permanently was akin to treason. My father remembers his brother Elí taking him aside shortly after he married my mother. "*Nos traicionaste*," Elí told him. "You broke up the family." In fact, the betrayal had happened many years before. The oldest sibling, Alfredo, left to seek his fortune when he was very young. He served as a mercenary in Pancho Villa's army while still in his teens. Somehow Alfredo managed to avoid being drafted during World

War I. In his twenties and before he married and moved out of the house on New Mexico Avenue, he joined the many Hispanos who sought seasonal employment in the fields and mines of Colorado. The rest of Angelina's children, however, were still living at home when Grandfather Teofilo died in 1935.

Ultimately, four of them lived out their lives on the original homestead. José, Elí, and Tito joined the military following Pearl Harbor. José and Elí returned home straightaway after the war ended and never left again. Tito, who followed my father in birth order, took his lead from Dad. He moved on after obtaining his bachelor's degree in 1947, the same year Dad was awarded his master's degree. Rolo and Lala never left the ancestral home.

Even in the case of the offspring who left, Grandmother Angelina maintained close ties with and a strong influence over them. At the onset of World War II, Alfredo moved to California to work in the war industries. Like many of his *paisanos*, he made California his home, but he remained in touch with his mother by mail and, in later years, by phone. After the war was over and domestic travel restrictions eased, he journeyed home often to visit her. My father and his brother Tito stayed in New Mexico. Dad moved to the upper reaches of the Rio Chama Valley, many miles and hours away from Las Vegas. Tito went to work for a state agency in Santa Fe. All three wrote their mother often. Tito, who lived closer, visited her regularly. I recall him scolding Dad for not writing or visiting his mother. Going through my father's correspondence following his death, I found a letter from Grandma written in 1941. In it, she chastised him for not coming home for Christmas.

I asked Lala once whether she had ever thought of leaving home. She was already in her seventies at the time of our conversation. As was the case with my father's responses, her answer was a long time coming, dragged up from memories preferably left untouched. "During the war they were recruiting teachers to work in Santa Fe," she said. "I was already twenty-one years old. Because I'd graduated from high school and had one year of college, I was an

excellent prospect." Her voice wistful, she told me: "But Mom wouldn't let me go." The familial compound was a metaphorical *fuerte*, one that kept the family in rather than intruders out.

PROTESTANT AND POOR

† † † My father, like his sister Myrtle, chose not to remember his early life. Looking back pained him. His only happy recollection was being his grandfather Albino's favorite. I, the beneficiary of my parents' relative privilege and affluence, wanted to know what his life had been like. "*Éramos muy pobres. Y de colmo, protestantes*," he said. Being poor and Protestant weighed on him. He ceased to be poor, but he never overcame the sense that economic disaster was around the corner. To that end, he made sure that the pantry was always stocked with canned goods, that there was always money in the savings account, that debt was paid off as soon as possible. However, my father remained a believing, practicing Protestant all his life.

When he cited his birth year, Dad always added that it was the year before New Mexico achieved statehood. His early life was very circumscribed: home, school, church. He loved trains. As a young man he would cross the Gallinas River to see the trains disgorging their passengers or to watch the engines being shunted at the roundhouse. On our infrequent visits to Las Vegas, he rose early and drove to New Town to see the Super Chief arrive and the freight trains lumber by.

"What did you do for fun?" I ask him on one of our trips together. "*Jugábamos a las canicas. Bailábamos trompos. Volábamos papalotes.*" Marbles, spintops, and kites. Things I also enjoyed as a child. "*Y echábamos perros a pelear*," he adds, grinning. My gentle, loving father liked to see dogs fight, stopped the car or interrupted whatever he was doing to see a dogfight. "One of my childhood friends came over one day," he recalls. "My siblings and I were out. My mother invited him in to wait for us. My friend sat in the kitchen while she did her chores. Bored and despairing of our return, he finally asked her, '*Doña Angelina, ¿no quiere echar perros a pelear?*' " He laughs, shaking his head at the thought of his mother's reaction to a child's invitation to set dogs to fighting.

Unlike me, my father did not love school. He and his siblings attended the local public school, where they were bullied and shunned because they were Protestants. And they had to look on when their more affluent classmates purchased candy and other treats at breaks and after school. "One day, on our way to school," he recounts in his usual low-key fashion, "my brother José clambered up on the roof of a house under construction. 'Look what I found in this bucket of nails,' he called down to us, waving a dollar bill. We had a glorious day. We bought candy and soft drinks and flaunted them in front of our classmates. When we got home that afternoon, Mother was waiting for us at the door. '*¿Quién se llevó un dólar del trastero donde guardo mi dinero?*' she asked. We got a whipping that day." From the corner of my eye, I see his face. It is cocked sideways. He is looking down. His lips are tightly pursed but spread

wide, and his cheeks are scrunched up. We share the same expression, manifest when we encounter some complexity, learn of someone's dilemma, recall an unfortunate event, or feel regret.

My father and two of his siblings, Elí and Tito, one older, one younger, were sent off by train in 1926 to the Menaul School in Albuquerque. Homesick and unhappy, my father would stand behind Bennett Hall, his dormitory, and watch the Super Chief roll by on its way north. When he came home at Christmas break one of his peers interrogated him. *"¿No te pones triste?"* the friend wanted to know. "*Sí*," he responded. "*¿No te dan ganas de llorar?*" the friend persisted. "*Sí. Pero me las aguanto.*" He often felt like crying, he confessed, but resisted doing so. He had to put up a brave face for his younger brother Tito, who was even more miserable than he was.

The Menaul School was Dad's home for the next four years. The photo album he kept during that time documents fleeting moments of his life there. The snapshots are taken after church, at a school function, on an outing. In the former he is formally dressed: dark suit, white shirt, tie. Otherwise he sports dark trousers and a white shirt. Over time his face lost its soft, boyish roundness. Always good-looking, he became increasingly handsome. Many of the photos show him in the company of a young woman, equally dressed up. They were taken, he told me, on Sunday afternoons after church services, when he visited the Harwood School, a Methodist boarding school for young women.

My father returned to Las Vegas after graduating from high school in 1930 and worked as a carpenter's helper and busboy. Over the next year he advanced to waiting tables. Given the times, he felt he had a good situation. But, he added, "I realized soon enough that waiting on tables was not a way out of poverty." In the fall of 1932, in the middle of the Depression and with the aid of a personal loan his mother obtained, he crossed the Gallinas River into New Town and enrolled at New Mexico Highlands University, where he remained in college for the next three years.

Dad was closemouthed about his college days. His major was business education. I envied his ability to write in shorthand, and he was an excellent typist. But he also took courses in Spanish and English literature. He sometimes recited poems he had memorized. I came across some of them—Dario's "Juventud, divino tesoro" and Antonio Machado's "Caminante, no hay camino"—in my own studies and even used some of the novels, dramatic works, and poetry collections from his college courses in my own. Like him, I was partial to the Spanish writers of the turn of the century, the realists and naturalists as well as the Generation of '98 writers.

As children we read in Dad's college yearbook that he was a "thespian," which occasioned no end of giggles from us. My sister Concha, whom he was much closer to than me, ferreted out that acting was what he enjoyed most in college. His proudest moment, he told her, was playing the role of Don Juan in Tirso de Molina's *El Burlador de Sevilla*, in both its English- and Spanish-language productions.

Dad's university studies were interrupted in the summer of 1935 by the death of his father. That fall he left Las Vegas to take up full-time employment as a teacher. Over the course of the next two summers he completed the requirements for his bachelor's degree, which he was awarded in 1937. Thereafter he returned only to visit his family and to continue his studies. On one of those visits Concha, who also studied at Highlands University, took him on a drive around town. She told him she had loved her years at Highlands and Las Vegas and lamented that she had not been able to stay there. "*Yo no*," he told her. "I couldn't wait to leave. The only reason I return is family."

DOWNSTREAM, THEN UPSTREAM AGAIN

† † † When my father left Mills and moved downstream to Luna County and the community of Los Lunas, located on the banks of the Rio Grande below Albuquerque in August 1937, he reintegrated himself into a Hispano community. His fellow teachers were Hispanos, as were the school officials, and the two years he was there were happy and satisfying ones. His religion seems not to have been at issue. He established a close and longtime friendship with Teles Sánchez and came to know his brother, noted educator George Sánchez, author of *Forgotten People*, the pioneering study on the Hispano population of New Mexico.

Love and politics took my father away from Los Lunas. He met my mother, Gabriela Barela, when he returned to Las Vegas to continue his studies at Highlands University in the summer of 1936 following his first year of teaching at Mills. The *ancianos*, our elders, say, "*Dios los crea, pero ellos solos se juntan.*" God creates them, but they get together of their own accord. In my parents' case, however, God both created and brought them together.

"They were both Protestants?" my listeners often exclaim upon hearing my stories. It amuses me that this should come as a surprise. That is why they connected—because they were both *protestantes.* Members of marginal groups seek each other out. Mom crossed the Gallinas River to attend Sunday services at the Spanish Presbyterian mission church. She was the out-of-towner and was invited to Sunday dinner. Dad courted her over the year by letter and then in person in the summer of 1937, while he was completing work for his bachelor's degree.

I have snapshots of them on the campus that summer. He is strikingly handsome. His black hair is neatly parted, and he is dapper in his dark trousers and white shirt. His sleeves are slightly rolled. She is a lovely and exceptionally poised young woman. Her hairstyle is conservative but not old-fashioned. The dress she wears is elegant without being showy. Her demeanor is sweet.

My father traveled to my maternal grandparents' home in the Española Valley in 1937, during his first year at Los Lunas, to ask for her hand in marriage. They fed him and put him up for the night in the parlor, which was unheated. It was already November and cold. "I shivered all night," he liked to tell us, grinning wryly, "but I stuck it out and got permission to marry your mother." The wedding took place at her home in December. I never thought to ask whether it was a civil or religious ceremony. But this, as in everything they did, was a discreet affair, with only family present. Myrtle recalls that Tito drove her and Grandmother Angelina from Las Vegas to attend but that they returned home shortly after the ceremony.

During their first year of married life, my parents had the long-distance commuter marriage of a modern couple. When they married Mom held an appointive office, deputy county clerk of Rio Arriba County. Several months later she presented herself as a candidate for election to the post of county clerk. It fell on Dad to accommodate himself to her realities. After classes ended on Friday afternoons he drove north from Los Lunas to Tierra Amarilla, a dis-

tance of almost 200 miles. The paved road ended just outside Española, and the gravel base deteriorated as he went farther north.

One evening, on his way to visit Mom, he slid off the road and into the drainage ditch just north of Navajo Canyon, when Highway 64 still wound its way along the arroyo up to Canjilón before descending to La Cebolla. It was early spring, meaning it was still winter at the 7,500-foot elevation. He trudged up the frozen road along the *chamizal* past stands of piñon trees and Ponderosa pines, then made his way down into the little river valley. The new moon reflected on the snow, permitting him to avoid icy patches. He entered the only place where he saw any light, the Canjilón Bar. The conversation stopped, and every eye turned toward the stranger at the door. He was, he says, on the verge of turning around and walking out. But instead he explained his situation and, with the exception of Don Adolfo Maes, the proprietor, who stayed behind to mind the bar, all present piled into a truck, accompanied him back to his car, and pushed it out of the ditch. Before going on to Tierra Amarilla, my father

bought a round of drinks and shook hands with everyone. He ceased to be a stranger in Canjilón that evening.

At the end of the school year, Dad asked his friend Teles why his contract had not been renewed when his fellow teachers' had. Teles, a veteran of the system, asked him, "Have you been to see Judge Chávez and asked to be reappointed? *Hay que pedírselo a él.*" My father did so, out of necessity but with great resentment. His father, Teófilo, who unlike his peers was an educated man literate in both English and Spanish, had yearly been required to ask the local political boss for reappointment as a teacher in some rural school.

When my father left Los Lunas and his friends the following year, it was to take a job as an elementary teacher in a one-room school in a canyon on the banks of the Chama River, a few miles west of Tierra Amarilla. Unlike his father, who traveled to his job by horse or sulky, he drove daily in the Buick sedan he and my mother bought after they married. When the snows came in November, he parked the car at the lip of the canyon and walked down to the school. Afternoons he caught a ride back up the canyon on the sleigh Don Lionel Rodela used in the winter to deliver mail to the communities surrounding Tierra Amarilla.

The first thing he did to incorporate himself into the local culture was buy fishing tackle. During June and July 1938, he spent every afternoon on the river but came home empty-handed and, he said, frustrated enough to break his fly rod in two. In August, he, Mom, and some friends went on a pack trip up to the Brazos Meadows, located behind the Brazos Peak to the north of Tierra Amarilla. Crawling on his hands and knees up to one of the little brooks that crisscross the meadows, he dipped his baited hook into the water. When he felt a tug, he horsed the line, sending a tiny native trout flying into the tall grass behind him. Dad recounted the story with great glee, telling how he spent half an hour looking for the damned fish. But he was a persistent man, and by the following summer's end he had given up fishing with bait and become a capable fly fisherman.

Despite his urban background and inclinations, he also became a hunter. When he got lost in the mountains above Canjilón and his companions broke the axle of the Buick searching for him, he gave up hunting. He remained a dedicated fisherman, though, until late in life. My enduring memory of him is when he was already approaching eighty. Late on a July afternoon, as we were fishing the Pagosa River in southwestern Colorado, I turned to my son Carlos and asked him where his grandfather was. It was time to head home, and neither of us had seen him for a good while. As we were walking downstream toward our car, blinded by the setting sun, we saw him crawling across a railroad trestle. We stood, holding our breath, until he made it safely to the other side. Trout were rising on the riverbank opposite him, he later told us, and there was no other way to get there.

A FAMILY OF READERS

† † † When World War II ended my father returned to New Mexico Highlands University in Las Vegas to pursue a master of arts degree, and in subsequent years to renew his teaching and supervisory certificates. Except for the summer of 1946, when we all came with him and occupied an apartment adjacent to the Spanish Presbyterian mission church manse, my mother stayed in our home in Tierra Amarilla. Once my sister turned three, Mom worked year-round as an employee of the county or as a contract worker for an abstract firm, conducting real estate title searches. Dad attended the first of the two

summer sessions and stayed in Grandma's house. He took me with him, probably because Mom had her hands full with my younger siblings.

I was the first grandchild on both sides of the family and as such the beneficiary of the love and attention not only of grandparents but also of multiple aunts and uncles. Because of our home's proximity to their farm, I spent more time with my maternal grandparents. But when I was a child, it was Grandma Madrid's home in Las Vegas I loved to visit best. In Las Vegas there were no animals to feed, fields to hoe, or crops to harvest. There wasn't even any kitchen duty. Uncles Elí and Rolo cooked, set the table, and washed up after meals. They also cleaned the house and washed clothes.

The radio was on from early morning to late evening. I woke up to the news, followed by the morning programming of light music and variety shows. Later the local station, KFUN, switched to a program of Mexican music, which both Rolo and Elí listened to. The soap operas began after lunch and ended with the news hour. Seemingly oblivious to most programs on the radio, all listened intently when the news came on.

I was highly attuned, at a very young age, to the linguistic demands the larger society placed on Hispanos seeking to make their way in an English-speaking world. Grandmother Angelina's linguistic abilities fascinated me. She had achieved what was expected of us, what would make us truly acceptable. Her English was impeccable. She spoke it without a Spanish accent—no embarrassing long *eee* when short *ihhh* was called for, no telltale *ess* when *zzz* was required. Precise pronunciation. Perfect intonation. Divine diction.

By age ten I had an extensive fund of words and expressions. I read every magazine I came upon, as well as all the library books the traveling bookmobile made available to me. My parents owned an encyclopedia, and I read entire sections of it. Moreover, the social and professional worlds they inhabited exposed me to a considerable variety of discourses. But I was always captivated by Grandma's locutions—not just her choice of words, phrases, and expressions, but her style of speech. I loved to hear her exclaim, "Oh, my" and "For goodness' sake" and "Gracious me." It was out of her mouth that I first heard the words "confounded," "cantankerous," "discombobulated," "fortuitous," and "extraordinary." To a ten-year-old, it was quintessentially American. When she conversed with my father, Grandma alternated between English and Spanish, but with my siblings and me it was always English. Outside the home and beyond the neighborhood, whether shopping, visiting, or driving around, English was de rigueur.

Spanish was the lingua franca of the household, however. My grandmother spoke with my uncles and my Aunt Myrtle in Spanish, especially when she asked them to do something. Rolo and José always spoke Spanish. Elí, Myrtle, and Tito used Spanish and English interchangeably. My siblings and I learned to move back and forth between languages depending on the person and the situation.

Grandma was just as precise in her use of Spanish as she was of English. Spanish was the language of the religious services at the Old Town mission church, which we attended whenever we visited Las Vegas. I grew up with both the English and Spanish versions of the Lord's Prayer and the Doxology, as well as of my favorite hymns. I don't believe I ever had reading instruction in Spanish as a child, but I could read the Spanish-language hymnal at an early age. Curiously, I do not recall any Spanish-language literature, religious or otherwise, around the house. At my maternal grandparents' farm most printed materials were in Spanish, but in the Madrid household all were in English.

The Madrids were a family of readers. Lala remembers coming home from school for lunch and finding her mother sitting in front of the stove with her feet on the oven door, reading away, oblivious to the hour. Grandma subscribed to *Family Circle* and *Good Housekeeping* and brought home past issues of *Life*, *Look*, *Collier's*, and the *Saturday Evening Post* from her employer's home. Dad picked up the latest issue of *Time* on his way home from his classes.

Lala favored movie and romance magazines. Elí had a stack of dime novels by his bedside, mysteries and westerns. José, who subscribed to *Popular Mechanics* and *Popular Science*, read the local newspaper, the *Optic*, and then worked out the crossword puzzle. Uncle Rolo read the paper and paged through whatever magazine was handy. But I liked Lala's choices best and read them cover to cover.

I had the run of the family compound, including the *fuerte*, the log house bunker where Elí slept. He allowed me to read his paperbacks in the cool of the *fuerte*. Between chores we played twenty-one and penny-ante poker, using the jar of pennies Grandma kept in the china cupboard. Rolo, despite his hermetic character and laconic nature, answered my endless questions. He also made a slingshot for me, the first one I ever had. Tito allowed me to tag along when he went to town on errands. José was his usual grumpy self when he got home, but he always brought treats from the grocery store where he worked: peanut butter crackers, cokes, candy, magazines, and the latest cereals: Kix, Frosted Flakes. Grandma was partial to fruit: bananas, grapes, Bing cherries, melons. When peaches came into season, she sliced them and served them with ice cream.

My fondest memories are of Lala. She radiated the beauty of the women I saw in her movie magazines. The first perfume scent I remember was the one I smelled on her when she hugged me on arriving home from work, before she changed into her housedress. I sat and listened to her chatter as she helped Grandma in the kitchen and set the table for supper. When I tried to join in, she and Grandma laughed with delight at my childish inanities.

On Sunday mornings Lala played the piano at church. I sat in the pew with Dad and Grandma and watched her closely. She was elegant in the simplicity of her Sunday best, and her fingers flowed over the keys with assurance. I sang the hymns along with Grandma and Dad, noting how she made sure the congregation stayed with her.

After dinner, while my uncles cleaned up and Grandma and Dad were otherwise occupied, I sat with Lala on the front porch as she smoked a cigarette. Afterward we listened to her latest record purchase or to the radio. Unlike my uncles, who listened to Mexican music on KFUN, she preferred American pop music. At night we listened together to country music, swing, and hit parade tunes while she did her nails, brushed her hair, or read magazines.

Even at a young age, I found it curious that visitors to the Madrid compound were rare. I was used to people coming by my parents' home in Tierra Amarilla, whether friends, colleagues, constituents, or visiting dignitaries. Out-of-town officials came over for dinner when district court was in session. The people who hired Mom to carry out document searches came to our home to conduct their business. My parents held an annual party for my father's faculty, usually before the Christmas holidays. Along with their close friends, they took turns hosting poker parties.

I am sure that Don Gabino Rendón, the minister, came by, but never during my extended stays. We saw Dad's cousin, Carlos Madrid, and his family at church, but only his wife, Alice, stopped by, always on an errand. Rolo said cousins Carla, Sylvia, and Paula came by from time to time, but not while I was visiting. The only persons who entered the compound regularly were Veronica, who helped out with household chores, and her son Silviano, known in the family as Dopey, who was my playmate when I visited.

Elí and Rolo left the compound only on weekend evenings. Out the back entrance, which took them down the lane and past the church, then down the hill and, I imagine, toward the Old Town plaza and the commercial area that stretched east toward the Gallinas River and New Town. After dinner, on Fridays or Saturdays, as I played in the backyard, Lala emerged from the house and, like her brothers, headed down the lane. She was dressed very differently than usual, not unlike the movie stars in her magazines. As she walked up the rise to the lane leading toward Old Town I would call out, "*¿Adónde vas, Lala?*"

"*A farolear*," she would answer, laughing. *Farolear*, from *farol*, meaning a lantern. I imagined her moving through space, emitting bursts of light, not unlike the glowworms we watched as we sat on the front porch in the evenings. *Farolear*. It remains to this day the most poetically redolent word I have ever heard. Someday, I thought to myself as she disappeared into the dusk, someday I, too, will go out *a farolear*.

THE GARDEN AT THE EDGE OF THE PRAIRIE

††† I was usually asleep when Dad and Tito left the house to attend classes. José left for work even earlier. Lala left while I was still rubbing the sleep from my eyes at the kitchen table. Elí and Rolo were usually sitting in the kitchen, enjoying a smoke and listening to the radio between chores. Rolo spoke only when spoken to, but Elí interrogated me while I had breakfast. What had I learned in school? What did my grandparents have for breakfast? Did I have a girlfriend yet? Like Tito, asking questions and teasing seemed to be his way of engaging. While he talked, he checked to see that the bean pot had sufficient water and turned over the green chiles he was roasting on the stove. Elí and Rolo mostly stayed at home, except when they went to sweep the church or weed the churchyard.

After breakfast I wandered out of the house. Grandma was usually in her flower garden. She greeted me warmly and asked whether I had slept well. I sat in the sun warming myself while she puttered. Her gardening outfit was a thin print dress, overlaid with an equally thin apron, cloth gloves, and a straw hat that she tied under her chin. Her footwear consisted of worn, low-cut tennis shoes that were frequently untied. Next to reading, gardening was her favorite activity. She loved flowers, knew their names, studied garden magazines, transplanted cuttings, and sought out new varieties.

The only things that grew in our yard in Tierra Amarilla were hollyhocks and *rosas de Castilla*. Mom kept potted geraniums indoors. My maternal grandmother's tiny garden on the farm in Española, though relegated to the north side of the farmhouse in a space inhospitable to row crops, had the advantages of lower elevation, rich floodplain soil, and ample water. Alongside lilac and rose bushes grew irises, dahlias, zinnias, and, most memorably, a single poppy plant with blooms whose color matched the vibrant orange of the Sangre de Cristo sunsets. Wild mustard and alfalfa competed for space with the flowering plants, and various other weeds insinuated themselves wherever there was a patch of soil.

Grandmother Angelina's garden, in contrast, was located on the arid eastern Sangre de Cristo piedmont, more than 1,000 feet higher than the Española Valley. Elí and Rolo had terraced the sloping front yard, which was oriented west toward the mountains and away from the prairie. Over the years José and Dad carted compost and topsoil from the surrounding countryside to enrich its anemic soil. Unlike my maternal grandmother's somewhat haphazard garden, Angelina's was laid out geometrically, terrace by terrace. The flowering plants were spaced two to three feet apart. Each species was centered in an earthen trough, to hold water. Although the aridity helped keep weeds in check, Rolo patrolled the garden daily with his hoe.

My range of floral knowledge is limited, although I can now tell a petunia from a pansy. But the names of the flowers in my grandmother's garden still resonate much as they did when she identified them for me: phlox, asters, foxglove, mallows, azaleas, delphiniums, nasturtiums, chrysanthemums. My sister Concha, as a four-year-old, was

entranced by Grandma's garden and followed her around as she watered the plants individually. Concha subsequently became the gardener of the family, but both Elí and Lala teased her for years, recalling that she kept asking, "Is this a gardenia, Grandma?" Lala and Rolo continued to reside there a century after the family moved upstream. They kept the garden up for a few years after Grandma's death in 1958, but except for the irises and hollyhocks that require no tending, no other flowers are in evidence.

CAST OUT OF THE GARDEN

† † † There was a moment, all too brief, when I was the center of the family's attention, the one and only grandchild. That ended when my brother Ibáñez was born three years later. Nene, as he came to be known, was an adorable child to whom every possible endearment stuck: cute, darling, lovable, sweet, rascally, mischievous, and, in later life, charming and delightful. Even the birth of the first granddaughter, Concha, did not dislodge him from that central space. He merely shared it with her.

My displacement did not occur to me until some years later, when I sensed that Grandmother Angelina had withdrawn her affection from me. I was ten years old. I can't offer any proof. Children just know these things. Grandma had made the long bus trip from Las Vegas to our home in Tierra Amarilla that summer to visit. We were all waiting for her in front of Straus's Mercantile Store. She got off the bus, kissed my younger siblings and exclaimed over them, but scarcely acknowledged me. I was troubled enough to complain about it to my friend Ernesto, not something a ten-year-old would normally do.

I must have taken it up with my mother as well. She told me that Grandma had said to her, "*Tienes un hijo muy criticón.*" Allegedly I found fault with everything. I certainly was a *sábelotodo*, a know-it-all, and an *entremetido*, a busybody. Being so drove my teachers crazy. My maternal grandmother called me a

fisgón because I was always poking into everything. But I don't recall being disliked by my teachers or grandmother as a consequence. I suspect Grandma's remark was an *indirecta*, a shot. She was saying that I took after my mother's side of the family. In any case I believed my Grandmother Angelina had taken a dislike to me.

The distance between Tierra Amarilla and Las Vegas did not lend itself to weekend visits, and our trips to my father's family home were infrequent. My mother only occasionally came along and never during holidays. Her excuse was that she was needed on the farm, but I overheard her on some occasion complain to her sisters that her brothers-in-law Elí and José were always finding fault with her. "*Son muy criticones*," she said. Clearly finding fault was a Madrid family trait.

Except for holiday visits, I don't recall spending much time in Las Vegas after I was ten. By the next year I was helping out on my maternal grandparents' farm. If I went to Las Vegas during the summer, it was because Dad had arranged a visit to the dentist. While I missed the idyllic quality of my early visits, José, Elí, Rolo, and Lala were as loving and attentive as ever. The icebox and subsequently the refrigerator were always full of cokes. Grandma still peeled fresh peaches and served them with ice cream.

I do have loving memories of Grandma Madrid past my eleventh birthday: digging up wild columbine in the Sangre de Cristo foothills to transplant in her garden; singing along with her at religious services; laughing with her at something my siblings said; hearing her say something in English that I had only experienced in written form; observing that she too always had her nose in a book, or magazine, or newspaper. But I never felt as close to her, even as I wanted her love and attention, and her approval. She had imprinted me deeply, and despite her sense that I tilted toward the Barela clan, I was most markedly a Madrid.

MY FATHER ENTERS HISTORY

††† In the fall of 1940 my father obtained an appointment in the high school in Tierra Amarilla, becoming the school's first lay teacher. The high schools of Rio Arriba County were exclusively staffed by nuns from various orders, as were many of the elementary schools. This phenomenon was the legacy of the century-long struggle between Hispanos and Anglos for control over the society and its institutions, played out in multiple arenas—electoral and appointive offices, churches, schools, irrigation districts.

My father's supervisor at Tierra Amarilla High School was the Mother Superior of the Oldenburg Order of Franciscan Nuns, Sister Mary Eva, whom he respected deeply. He also grew very fond of some of his fellow teachers—Sister Mary Genevieve, Sister Mary Virginia, and Sister Mary Catherine, among others—and they in turn became fond of him. His appointment called for him to teach typing, shorthand, accounting methods, and Spanish, but he also coached basketball and football into the late 1940s. Despite being an outsid-

er, he fit in well, was highly respected by students and their parents, and was known to one and all as Mr. Madrid.

Following our trip to Mills, I asked whether the locals had harassed him when he was serving as coach. He laughed and shook his head. "If anybody had tried to," he said, "Sister Mary Eva would have been on them like a terrier."

His older cousin, the Rev. Manuel Madrid, won office as president of the school board of the Mora County Public Schools in order to wrest control of the schools from a Catholic religious order. He later served as the superintendent of the county's schools. Unlike him, my father did not challenge the status quo. He sought only to be a good teacher and a respected member of his community, and to avoid being subjected to arbitrary authority.

My father entered history half a century after his grandfather Albino, and in both cases religion was at the heart of the matter. In the fall of 1948, eight years after he began teaching at Tierra Amarilla High School, he became the first lay principal of a Rio Arriba County public school. His appointment occurred as a consequence of a U.S. Supreme Court ruling that forced religious personnel out of New Mexico's publicly funded school systems. Dad had the support of lay and religious leaders alike, even though he was the community's lone practicing *protestante*. He served as principal of the Tierra Amarilla public schools until 1955, then later of two other Rio Arriba County schools. His career as a school administrator was not without its challenges, but they were driven by the political motivations of school board members and superintendents, not by religious or racial and ethnic considerations.

Ironically, the heretic and interloper found community where he probably least expected it, in a predominantly Catholic and rural part of the Rio Arriba. His charges, having graduated, invited him to their weddings and the baptismal ceremonies of their offspring. The miscreants, usually male, who had enlisted or been drafted into military service returned in time to seek his counsel and wisdom concerning the larger world. More than one of his students became a colleague.

On his eightieth birthday, almost three decades after he and Mom had left Tierra Amarilla permanently, I gave my father the book *Community and Continuity: The History, Architecture, and Cultural Landscape of La Tierra Amarilla*, a beautiful study by cultural geographer Chris Wilson. Dad had relocated for the seventh time and was living with my brother Ibáñez in Albuquerque following the death of my mother. It was, I told him, a study of our home community. "Yes," he said, "yes," repeating himself as he did when he felt strongly about something. "It was and remains home."

Unlike his memories of Mills, he looked back at his time in Tierra Amarilla with affection. And in contrast with his trips to Las Vegas, he returned to Tierra Amarilla happily and as often as he could, to fish, to visit longtime friends, to have a beer and catch up with local gossip at Dan's saloon, as well as to attend funeral services. When he no longer drove long distances I arranged my

schedule to take him from Rio Abajo country to the Rio Arriba to visit friends and relatives, whose numbers diminished yearly. Over lunch at JoAnn's Cafe in Española, just short of my father's eighty-fifth birthday, I saw him grimace, an expression I recognized as sadness mixed with resignation. "*Ya no sé por qué vengo. Ya no conozco a nadie.*" I protested that it was important for him to keep returning, that he still had friends and colleagues in the area, as well as members of Mom's family, who loved him dearly. We stood, and as I walked to the cash register I heard voices from three separate tables call out, "Mr. Madrid!"

THE SCENTS OF HOME

† † † As soon as classes end in the spring, I drive to New Mexico to flee the heat and humidity of San Antonio. My trip takes me along the southern edge of the Hill Country and into the mesas and plains of West Texas. Past the town of Junction the flora begins to change. Shrubs and cacti replace oak trees. Dis-

tant buttes become visible long before I reach them. Even the labels of the topography change. Instead of sloughs and creeks, the road maps mark arroyos and cerros. The landscape and the atmosphere are not unlike those of my New Mexico *querencias*, the places I always seek to return to. When I alight from my car to stretch, the air is hot and dry. My eyes itch; my nasal passages shrivel. There are no smells, except for the slightly unpleasant whiff issuing from the trash can as I dump my waste, the fumes emitted by trailer trucks as they pull away, or the tang of urine as I relieve myself. I have left behind the odor-infused humidity of South Texas and entered the arid zones of my childhood and adolescence.

In arid zones one can only smell very pungent odors, usually those associated with decay and defecation. The presence of water, however, increases the range and intensity of smells. For the peoples who inhabit arid environments there is no more memorable and pleasurable odor than that of wet earth, particularly earth moistened by rain. I can still conjure up the smell of the spring runoff on Nutritas Creek, just a couple of hundred yards from our home in Tierra Amarilla. It was the smell of life and death. Life because spring was on its way. The peepers sang *viva voce* at nightfall. A reddish tint on the willows lining the river slowly displaced the winter dullness of accumulated driftwood. Death because, inevitably, a calf, a lamb, or a colt had been surprised by the flood current, and its carcass was now trapped under a log at river's edge.

There were other no less memorable odors, some of which I continue to experience when I visit the spaces of my youth: piñon wood burning, sagebrush after a rain, Russian olive trees in bloom. The most familiar, most pleasurable, are the domestic ones: beans boiling on the stove, green chiles roasting on the griddle, piñon nuts toasting in the oven, pork sizzling in the pan.

The odors associated with my maternal grandparents' farm, a place that by virtue of being near the Rio Grande was much more humid than the high, dry place I called home, have embedded themselves in my senses. When I drive on I-10 in late summer, I have a sensory experience worthy of Proust as I approach Balmorhea. The Pecos River runs a few miles to the north, and on the fields along its narrow valley farmers grow melons—honeydews, musks, Persians, and, above all, cantaloupes.

The honeyed, earthy smell of cantaloupes transports me back to the family farm, and other smells surface: the yeasty odor of the bread my grandmother baked twice weekly in her outdoor oven; the lime-infused smell of corn being processed in copper vats for posole and *chicos*; the complex scents issuing forth from containers in the storeroom, which held wheat flour, cornmeal, ground barley, chile powder and chile pods, and dried apples and apricots, as well as gasoline, kerosene, and insecticides.

CANICAS

† † † I am already partially awake when I hear my grandmother Trinidad's voice calling to me from the foot of the stairs. The screeches and slaps of the kitchen screen door opening and closing have roused me from sleep. I peek out the window. It is still dark in the shade of the house, but I hear my grandfather carrying out his early morning chores below. The only visible light is that of the rays of the rising sun on the topmost leaves of the cottonwoods, which rustle in the morning breeze. The 7:30 whistle signals the beginning of the workday at Cook's Lumber Yard while I am lacing up my shoes. I smell bacon frying.

As I enter the kitchen, Grandma greets me. "*¿Cómo amaneciste?*" she asks. It is a familiar greeting, used by family and friends. Not the inquiry in English that asks about sleep, but rather the Hispano greeting that asks about waking. "*Bien, Grandma, ¿y usted?*" I answer. My aunt Aurora, who is fixing a lunch to take to school, looks up. Unlike her, I am on school holiday. I am bent over the washbasin when my grandfather Ramos enters the kitchen. "*Buenos días te de Dios*," he says to me. "*Ven ayúdame*," he adds as he turns to exit. Around his family my grandfather was a man of few words, and they were usually commands. We knew better than to dally.

I follow him out. One of his sows is sick. He has decided to take it to the veterinarian, in Santa Fe, and I am to go with him. The sow squeals loudly as I help him load it in the back of his truck. Oso and Güero, the farm dogs, are frantic with excitement. I shoo Güero away. He doesn't know how hard Grandpa can kick. We return to the kitchen and wash our hands, then sit down to breakfast.

Before every meal my grandfather offered the blessing. He waited until we were seated and quiet before he began. I listened carefully. He always began his prayers in the same way, addressing the Lord and thanking him for giving us one more day of life: *Nuestro Dios, Padre y Señor, gracias te damos por este día* . . . And they always ended the same way, invoking the Trinity: *Esto te lo pedimos en el nombre del Padre, del Hijo, y del Espíritu Santo.* But in between, quietly and mainly in monotone, my grandfather gave thanks for the food that lay before us, for the hands that had prepared it, and for the Lord's bounty; asked God to have mercy on the poor, the infirm, the unfortunate; commended relatives and friends who had passed away; and sought the Lord's blessing for loved ones at home and away. If someone were ill God's intervention was sought; if some misfortune had come to his attention he asked for God's mercy; if there were visitors their names were included in the prayer. My grandfather addressed Him with the familiar *tú* form, yet the relationship was a respectful one. The prayer was delivered on behalf of us all and as if God were in our presence, listening. As a child I dared not open my eyes or look up, for fear that might be the case. I loved the words—*siervos*, *socorro*, *corporales*, *misericordias*. They were not words we used every day, but they were familiar to me from the prayers. When my grandfather finished we all said—did not mumble, but rather said—*Amén.*

While my grandfather gets himself ready for our trip, I exit the kitchen into

the patio. I sit in the *resolana*, the area exposed to the morning sun. The apricot tree my grandparents planted when they moved from Las Truchas to San Pedro provides shade in the summer months. During the rest of the year the adobe walls of the house catch and hold the heat. My brother Ibáñez and I play *canicas*, marbles, in the hard-packed soil of patio almost year-round. The dogs are lying in a patch of sun next to the bench. Oso, shaggy and bearlike, pays me no mind. This is his space. I am interloping. Güero, a handsome Irish setter who showed up on the farm the previous fall, curls up next to me.

From the patio I can survey most of my grandparents' farm. In the melon field to the east, the vines have wilted and the ripening honeydews are now fully exposed to the sun. To the south, the last of the peppers are turning a mottled purple. By the end of the week they will be a bright red, carmine, like the Avon lipstick Mom sells. In the orchard the leaves are turning, and their green and brown hues highlight the reds and yellows of the maturing fruit. The bright yellows of the pear trees stand out among the darker shades of the apple trees. To the east, above the trees that line Lower San Pedro Road, I can see the tips of the Truchas Peaks. They are already covered with snow.

I get up when my grandfather comes out of the kitchen. He is dressed in the clothes he wears when he leaves the farm on business: khaki pants and a khaki shirt, stiff with starch and neatly pressed. His shirt is buttoned at the neck and wrists. He has put on the Stetson and the shoes he wears to church and political rallies. As we head out the lane toward Highway 84, which will take us to Santa Fe, Grandpa stops to inspect the irrigation gate on the Lower San Pedro ditch. He is the *mayordomo*, the water boss for the local irrigation district. The *parciantes*, members of the district, all know him as Don Ramos and seek him out as he makes his rounds. Some request water. Others seek information or work. Once in a while someone will ask his advice on a legal matter. He served for many years as a justice of the peace and knows the law. The older ones, with time on their hands, want to talk about politics or about the latest local *pleitos* stemming from misunderstandings, disagreements, and feuds. *Mentir*, says my grandfather, which means to fib. He enjoys it himself. Away from the house he is talkative. He does not, however, discuss religion with his Catholic neighbors.

It is no different today. Two younger men pull up in a coupe with Utah plates. They are looking for work. My grandfather asks where he can find them if something comes up. Several locals who happen by ask him for water to extend their chile and tomato crop a few more days. He gives them an hour and a time and writes them into the notepad he keeps in his shirt pocket. Our neighbor Don Antonio looks up from his chores and walks over to join the conversation. A couple more trucks pull up.

I listen to their talk about the upcoming election. All favor or predict victory by *el general Eisenhower*, but my grandfather tells them he will vote the party ticket. He is a New Deal Democrat, has served as precinct chair on more than one occasion. Don Antonio wants to know about his apple crop. My grandfather says the one in the main orchard is excellent, but in the one bordering on Don Antonio's property the apples are small and scarred. "*La golpeó el granizo y luego no crecieron.*" Don Antonio commiserates. He has the same situation. I remember the hailstorm in June. It missed our farm but damaged the crops in the surrounding area.

Grandpa finally takes his leave, and we head down Lower San Pedro Road. Our neighbor Doña Celestina is sitting in a patch of sun, stringing ripening peppers into *ristras*. Her son Ramón is stripping corn and setting the ears out to dry. Grandpa stops from time to time to make sure no one is siphoning off water. Dogs come out of the adjoining yards and chase the truck ferociously as we drive by. Satisfied that they have scared us off, they prance grandly back to their *querencias*, their zones of comfort.

After he inspects the main gate where the waters are divided between the Upper and Lower San Pedro ditches, we head out again. At the intersection of Highway 84, instead of heading southeast, toward Santa Fe, my grandfather turns left, toward town across the Santa Cruz River bridge. It is a quiet morning. There is a cattle truck parked in front of Hedges' truck stop. The parking lot for Matilda's Café is empty.

We head north on the Taos highway and stop at Million's Electric. Grandpa needs two light fixtures and a plug, he tells me. Mr. Million knows us from my grandparents' church, where he has served as a greeter and usher for as long as I can remember. I tell him what we're looking for, and he retreats into the storage area. "This what you need?" he asks on his return. My grandfather nods and says, "How much?"

We return the same way we came, but instead of heading south for Santa Fe we fork west over the Rio Grande bridge into Española. We pass the Morris Chevrolet agency, Evans's Drugstore, and Cook's Lumber Yard and pull up at the Rio Arriba State Bank. It is not yet ten o'clock. Grandpa has been killing time, waiting for the bank to open. Across the street and down the road stands

my grandparents' church, the Evangelical United Brethren Church of Española.

My grandfather crosses the street to Hunter's Ford Motor Company. I join him. Mr. Hunter, a short, chunky man who reminds me of Jiggs in the *Maggie and Jiggs* comic strip, comes out and greets him. He and Mrs. Hunter are members of the Santa Cruz Evangelical United Brethren congregation across the Rio Grande. "You let me know when you are ready to buy, Mr. Barela. I'll offer you a good deal," Mr. Hunter says. My grandfather grins and nods, saying, "Okay, okay." Not likely, I think to myself. My grandfather likes Chevrolets.

As we enter the bank, Mr. Brasher, the bank president, greets him from behind his desk. A tall, elegant man who reminds me of Cary Grant, Mr. Brasher is also a member of my grandparents' church and teaches my Sunday school class. My grandfather doffs his hat and says, "Guden morn, guden morn." His favorite teller, the only bank employee who speaks Spanish, opens her window and says, "*Buenos días le de Dios, Don Ramos.*" It is a greeting used by the *ancianos*, the elders. They ask God's blessing on the listener. My grandfather makes a withdrawal and asks for his balance. While he transacts his business, I examine the artworks on the walls. They are reproductions of New England landscapes—white churches surrounded by picket fences, stone walls and cemeteries, village greens, oak and maple trees in autumn colors.

The land surrounding the Rio Grande Valley is bare and eroded. Clumps of grass grow here and there, as do ocotillo cactus, sagebrush, and stunted juniper. By contrast, the cottonwoods, fruit trees, row crops, and alfalfa fields located along the Rio Grande and its feeder valleys appear thick and lush. As we climb out of the Rio Grande Valley on our way to Santa Fe, I look east toward the Sangre de Cristo range. From the top of the hill I can see the entire Rio Santa Cruz Valley and its small *placitas*: Chimayó, Plaza Abajo, Ranchos, Cuarteles, Santa Cruz de la Cañada, La Puebla. Grandpa had land in La Puebla at one time. I ask him why he sold it. "*Porque nunca podía aprovechar la cosecha*," he answers. Someone always beat him to the harvest. They came in at night and cleaned the crop out.

We arrive at the veterinarian's shortly before eleven. My grandfather asks me to tell the receptionist we have a sick sow and find out if we should unload it. She exits the room, and when she returns she tells us the doctor will be out to examine it shortly. When the vet appears, he and I join my grandfather in the truck bed. The vet asks what the symptoms are. Grandpa explains, and I translate. "Swine fever," the vet says. He extracts a syringe from his kit and injects the sow. Back in the office he hands me a bottle of medication to add to the water and asks me how much water the trough holds. I estimate eight gallons. My grandfather says, "*No, sólo un galón*," and holds one finger up. I flush but do not contradict him. The vet looks at both of us. I look away. "Well, which is it?" he asks. I shrug.

As we leave town, I explain to my grandfather that the vet wanted to know how much water the feeding trough held. He looks at me sheepishly and tells me he thought the vet wanted to know how much water the sow drank. At the top of the hill he turns the wheel over to me. We arrive back in the valley just as the noon whistle releases Mr. Cook's employees to lunch. I start to turn left off the highway toward the farmhouse, but my grandfather tells me to keep going. He has spotted a trailer truck with Texas plates parked in front of Matilda's Restaurant.

I pull up next to the cab. The markings on the door read Amarillo Freight

Lines. The driver sits at the wheel, his elbow resting on the window frame. The hair on his forearm is reddish blond. When he turns toward us, I notice that his eyes are a yellowish-brown. My grandfather lowers his window. "Guden emen," he says. It is his English equivalent of *buenas tardes*, the standard greeting offered after the noon hour. "You buy apples?" my grandfather asks. The driver nods and then asks, "*¿Cuántas tienes?*" His response takes us by surprise. Unlike the local Anglos he speaks Spanish. My grandfather tells him the crop is large enough to fill half his truck. "*¿Dónde?*" the driver asks. Right across the river, my grandfather tells him, motioning with his chin. "*Vamos a verlas*," the driver commands us as he dismounts from his cab and jumps into the bed of our truck. The sow squeals, but he pays her no mind.

We pull up at the orchard and get out. My grandfather starts to open the gate, but our prospective buyer has leapt over the fence. Amarillo is tall and lanky. He wears jeans, boots, and a tailored western shirt but, unlike my grandfather, no hat. The shirt is open at the neck, and his sleeves are rolled to his elbows. His face, neck, and arms are sunburned and freckled. He strides down the rows, looking at the trees. "*¿Cuánto quieres por ellas?*" he asks. He speaks Spanish like we do. "*Tres pesos el cajón*," my grandfather responds. Amarillo shakes his head and offers $2.25 a box. He reaches up and picks an apple. "*Canicas*," he says. The apples are small, but not as small as the marbles my brother and I play with. "*Y golpeadas*," he adds. They have been bruised by hail. My grandfather smiles and says, "*Bueno*, $2.50." Amarillo nods, and my grandfather tells him to give us an hour to round up some help.

Amarillo is waiting for us when we return. We are halfway through the orchard when my aunt Aurora shows up with cold water and a tin of cookies. Güero is with her. He ignores me, runs up to Amarillo, and nuzzles him, tail wagging excitedly. Then he lies down under the truck. We take a short break, but Amarillo does not join us. He has his own water and nourishment in the cab of the truck. I watch him with interest. I have been in contact with Anglo

Texans since I was a child, whether cowpunchers, loggers, roughnecks, or tourists. We are wary of them. "*Los diablos tejanos*," say the *ancianos*, the old men who hang around the courthouse where my mother works. "*Canicas*," Amarillo sneers as he empties another crate of apples into the truck and marks it down on the notebook we are using to keep tab. My grandfather pays him no mind. When we return to the task he tells us, "*Pepenen parejo, parejito*." We are to strip the trees bare. I join Aurora. The two young men Grandpa contracted to help are teasing and laughing. She blushes and talks to me more than usual.

We finish stripping the orchard long after the whistle at Cook's has signaled the end of the day. My grandfather pays the help while Aurora and I load the ladders, crates, harnesses, and pouches into the truck. Amarillo is up on his truck, covering the fruit with a canvas tarp. My grandfather asks me to add up the markers. The total is 264 crates. Aurora checks my addition. It is correct. Then she picks up the water jugs and heads across the field for home. Güero, however, does not respond to her call. "*Me gusta tu perro*," Amarillo tells my grandfather. Grandpa nods and says, "*Es perro fino*." Güero is a pedigree dog. He tells Amarillo that Güero showed up at the farm last fall, hungry and bedraggled. "*Te doy quince pesos por él*," Amarillo offers. "*Vale*," my grandfather says. It's a deal. I'm sad but not surprised. I learned early on not to get attached to farm animals. Rabbits, kid goats, and calves get butchered regularly, and I am party to the slaughter.

Amarillo tells my grandfather he has to get a wire trans-

fer at Evans's Drugstore to pay him. My grandfather nods and tells him I will come along to collect the money. He has cows to milk and animals to feed. They do not exchange any pleasantries. I follow Amarillo into Española. At this hour the town police are having dinner, and there is no one around to pull me over. We park in front of the Granada Hotel across from the drugstore. While he conducts his business I page through the new *Collier's* magazine. Amarillo calls out, "Son, come over here." They are the first words I hear him speak in English. It is a familiar accent and manner, however. Bossiness seems to come naturally to the Anglo Texans we come in contact with. "*Nacen mandando*," the old ones say. They are born giving orders. I walk over to the counter. Mr. Evans, the pharmacist, recognizes me and nods. Amarillo counts out $550 and hands it to me. I don't take it. "The total was 264 boxes, and that adds up to $594," I tell him, my heart pounding. He shakes his head and says, "I'm paying you for 244 boxes. You tell the *viejo* that the other twenty were *canicas*. Take it or leave it." He hands me the money again. I flush, but I take it. Then I turn and leave, feeling as if my heart and stomach have exchanged locations. As I step out of the drugstore, I see Güero waiting patiently in the cab of Amarillo's truck. He is silhouetted in the rays of the setting sun, which highlight his reddish-brown coat. I turn around and say, "And the dog?" Amarillo makes a face and counts out another $15.

When I get home, my grandfather is finishing up his chores. Aurora is with him. Her eyes are red. She likes Güero, has made him her companion. "*¿Traes el dinero?*" my grandfather asks. I hand him the money and tell him what happened. He listens quietly. A sly smile appears on his face as he tells me, "*Está bien. Eran canicas.*" He explains that because of the hail damage, he didn't thin out the crop, and as a consequence the apples were small, like marbles. Unlike previous years, he says, "*No me chamuscó un troquero.*" Some trucker didn't come in and clean him out. "*Con esto me compro una troca nueva,*" he tells me as he counts out the money. With what he has in his bank account, it is enough to buy a new truck. Tomorrow I will go with him again, this time to the Morris Chevrolet agency. As we walk toward the kitchen, he puts his arm around me. I don't recall that he has ever done so before.

Dinner is waiting. We wash our hands and sit. My grandfather says grace. He asks the Lord to bless the food and the hands that prepared it, gives Him thanks for the day's bounty, and commends family and friends to Him. Grandpa ends his prayer with an expression of appreciation for my visit and for the help I provide. He regales us with stories and jokes. He tells one of my favorites, about simple-minded Brother Francisco, who always got the best of people who thought they were smarter than he was. Even my grandmother is smiling.

After dinner my grandfather reads *El nuevo mexicano*, the Spanish-language supplement to the *New Mexican*, aloud to us as Grandma and Aurora clean up. Then he sets up his account books on the kitchen table. Aurora sits down with him to do her homework. When she is done cleaning up Grandma sits down to read her Bible. There are no magazines in my grandparents' house, only my grandmother's religious tracts. Except for the Bible storybook she bought for me when I was younger, the only books are Grandpa's law books. I have reread the storybook several times, so I wander out to the kitchen patio. Oso looks up but doesn't otherwise move.

The sunset is reflected on the windowpanes of Doña Celestina's house. *Ristras* of ripe red chiles hang on the adobe walls facing south and west. On the roof I can see the ears of corn that have been set out to dry. As I sit there, the moon rises over the Sangre de Cristo range. It is a harvest moon, the color of the last of the honeydew melons lying out in the field before me. I watch it rise through the leafless branches of the apricot tree, its soft glow slowly replacing the rays of the setting sun.

THE ISLAND OF PROTESTANTS

† † † When my maternal grandparents, Ramos Barela and Trinidad Tafoya, moved downstream from Las Truchas, at the base of the Truchas Peaks, to the Rio Grande Valley, they were reversing the trajectory of their *antepasados*, who had moved upriver in stages from Santa Cruz de la Cañada and its environs more than a century earlier. Their Barela, Tafoya, López, Pacheco, Fernández, Rodríguez, and Sandoval ancestors were members of the historic Catholic community. Their baptisms are registered in the church records at Santa Cruz de la Cañada. Grandpa and Grandma were also baptized Catholic, as were their firstborn children, my mother, Gabriela, and her sister Nora. When they came downstream, however, they were *protestantes*. Their remaining offspring, Ernesto, Ramos Jr., Viola, and Aurora, were baptized at La Iglesia del Buen Pastor, the Presbyterian mission church in Las Truchas my grandparents belonged to.

The Barelas and Tafoyas, along with the families they subsequently married into, were forced to leave the original settlements along the Rio Grande at the

end of the eighteenth century when population growth outstripped available land resources. By the beginning of the nineteenth century, even Chimayó and Quemado, the communities of the upper Rio Santa Cruz Valley, were overpopulated. That left the valleys high on the western piedmont of the Sangre de Cristo range, already familiar to them because they were located on the high road to Taos. The highland valley known as Las Truchas was the one most immediate to residents of the Santa Cruz Valley, and that was where the offspring of the Barelas, Fernández, Tafoyas, and López families coincided.

A prolonged cold spell during the 1920s made farming and raising livestock at the 9,000-foot elevation, already a difficult undertaking, impossible. In 1929 my grandparents sold their land, stock, and equipment and bought a twelve-acre parcel in the parish of San Pedro, located at the confluence of the Rio Grande and the Rio Santa Cruz, across the river from Santa Clara Pueblo and catercorner from the town of Española. They farmed nine of those twelve acres intensively. On two they built a house, sheds, corrals, and pens. A one-acre marshy section served as a pasture for the milk cows and, before Grandpa bought a tractor, for the horses used to pull equipment. Seven acres were dedicated to money crops—chile, tomatoes, melons, and corn—on a large scale, and other garden crops—carrots, onions, radishes, cucumbers, and squash—on a smaller scale. On the remaining two acres my grandparents planted a variety of apple trees, as well as apricots, peaches, cherries, plums, and pears. It was a self-sufficient operation. The only foodstuffs they purchased were salt, sugar, flour, yeast, and spices such as cloves, vanilla, and cinnamon. Other than gas, oil, clothes, paper, seeds, insecticides, and hardware, the farm and farm animals provided everything.

The parcel my grandparents bought in San Pedro had previously been floodplain. They cleared and farmed the land right up to the sand and gravel beds of both rivers. Dams upstream prevented flooding under normal circumstances, but my grandparents grew anxious whenever there were high runoffs on either river. Their fields were under the aegis of the Santa Cruz Irrigation District, whose waters originated high in the Sangre de Cristo Mountains to the east.

If my paternal grandmother's home was a Protestant fortress under siege, my maternal grandparents' home was an island of Protestants in a sea of Catholics. It, too, was surrounded by water: to the west by the Rio Grande, to the north by the Rio Santa Cruz, and to the east and south by the irrigation ditches that fed the fields and orchards along the Rio Grande floodplain.

My uncles and aunts left the farm only to attend school, make a purchase for Grandma, or, before rural delivery, pick up the mail at the post office. Grandpa, however, came and went as his chores and obligations required.

Grandma left the island farm almost exclusively to attend religious services: Sunday worship and *la hora española* on Wednesday evenings. The only break in the farm routine was when family visited. She was always delighted to see her children, her grandchildren, and her Tafoya relatives. On those occasions she became highly animated, and her face took on an expression of sheer pleasure. The women would retire to the kitchen to prepare meals, exchange information, and tell stories, and on those occasions she talked and laughed with them.

The sole recurring absence from the farm took place on the Fourth of July, when the Barela-Tafoya family gathered at El Capulín, at Grandma's brother Celso's ranch. Grandma and her sister-in-law, Eloisa, sat and visited, pleased to be in each other's company and content to let their daughters and daughters-in-law attend to the food. Otherwise occasions away from the farm were spontaneous and brief. In the years before his untimely death in 1951, Tío Celso and Tía Eloisa would arrive at the farm unannounced on a midsummer day and say, "*A los baños!*" And off they went, having loaded cookware, provisions, mattresses, linens, and blankets in the truck bed, to enjoy the hot springs at Pagosa, Colorado, for a few days, leaving the farm in charge of my uncle Ernesto and my aunts Viola and Aurora.

Only family entered the compound, principally my grandmother's family, the Tafoya clan, who visited on a regular basis. The sole Barela who dropped by was a relative we knew as Primo Isidoro, who closed the café he owned across the Rio Santa Cruz on Sundays and walked over to visit after our midday meal.

In addition to being separated geographically from their fellow church members, my grandparents were set apart socially and culturally. They were tied to the soil, and thus to the Hispano Catholic community in whose midst they lived. Spanish, not English, was the language of their daily lives. They did not participate in the Anglo Protestants' social life, nor were they members of their professional organizations. Their paths crossed only in church or as a consequence of commercial or professional dealings.

On our frequent visits, my siblings and I attended Sunday school at my grandparents' church along with the youth of the Anglo congregation. I knew their last names. My grandparents purchased goods at their parents' establishments or used their parents' services. They embodied the larger world that

I was being taught, both implicitly and explicitly, I should be part of. I watched them closely and listened to them carefully. They were my window into a world I knew only through magazines, books, and the radio. All were cordial, and some were even friendly, but other than the contact we had through church I never entered their world, nor they mine. Home for me was elsewhere, and although I did not know where they lived, they certainly did not live in San Pedro.

Neither Viola nor Aurora had sustained social contact with any Anglos besides their teachers, so far as I was aware. Their social engagement was almost exclusively with my grandparents' families, and I never saw them interact with Anglos their age, either in or out of church. Ramos Jr., known to us as Ray, on the other hand, appeared to do so. Two of his classmates figure in my memory: Patty, daughter of the longtime superintendent of the McCurdy Mission School, and the man she would marry, Clarence, whose family owned a hardware store. Both were involved in putting together the fifth-year high school reunion along with Ray and his fiancée, Ruth Sánchez. I tagged along, happy to be in Ray and Ruth's presence, taking note of the ease with which Ray interacted with his peers, his teachers, and school officials.

I thought of Patty and Clarence, a handsome couple, as Ray's intimate friends. They do not, however, appear in the photos taken at Ray and Ruth's wedding. I suspect that they were principally classmates, and that because I saw them at church over the years they became part of my memory. When I asked Ray many years later, he did not recall the events I was describing. After school let out for the day, he told me, he headed home to help out and, as a consequence, had little or no interaction with his peers. Like me, he attended Sunday school as a child and adolescent, but after church the family returned home for dinner and the obligations of the farm.

The only other visitors to the farm were *parciantes,* members of the Lower San Pedro irrigation district, who came to petition for an allocation of water when Grandpa Barela was the mayordomo, the ditch boss. The petitioners pulled up to the large wooden ranch gate, not unlike boats pulling up to the dock. They honked and waited for Grandpa to come to the gate. If he was not around, Grandma came out of the house, drying her hands on her apron, to let them know where they might find him. Their business done, they backed their vehicles into the empty lot across the lane, turned around, and retraced their route to the Lower San Pedro Road.

MAYORDOMO DE AGUAS

† † † *Mayordomo de aguas.* I don't recall when I first heard the full title, but I do remember someone coming to my grandparents' farm and telling me: *Busco al mayordomo.* The mayordomo, or ditch boss, was Grandpa. He was in charge of parceling out the waters that irrigated the fields of San Pedro. The upper Rio Grande Valley was a land of no snow and little rain, and its farmers were thus dependent on the runoff from the mountains to the north and east.

Sin agua no hay vida, my grandmother was fond of saying. She was of even fewer words than my grandfather, some of which she spoke in aphorisms. My favorite was the one she voiced every morning when she put beans on to boil: *Sin frijoles no hay comida.* Beans were at the core of every meal. Although my grandparents bartered for pinto beans instead of growing them, I knew water was essential both for their growth and for preparing them.

I grew up mindful of water. Until my parents built their own home in Tierra Amarilla and dug a well to supply the household, the water used for washing, whether dishes, clothes, or floors, was drawn in buckets from ditches. Drinking water was obtained from hand-dug wells or carted in barrels filled from the springs that fed the fish hatchery in Los Ojos. As far back as I can remember, ditches were like a magnet I was pulled toward. Dandelions, the first sign of spring, appeared on their banks, followed by wild alfalfa, wild mustard, and sunflowers as summer finally arrived in the high country. Frogs emerged from

deep sleep to lay their eggs. Where the fast-moving water slowed, wispy water bugs danced on the surface. An occasional trout that had pursued a developing hatch downstream from the diversion dam wove its way rapidly back upstream on sensing movement on the bank.

The *acequia madre*, the mother ditch that brought water down from the dam upstream from Chimayó, split in two just south of Highway 84, which ran northwest from Santa Fe and through the Española Valley. One fork, the García ditch, provided water to the long-lot fields of Upper San Pedro, and the other, the Ciruelas ditch, also known as *la acequia de los Ortegas*, fed the fields of Lower San Pedro. Grandpa was in charge of the Lower San Pedro ditch. The runoff from the ditch emptied into the Rio Grande, to be recaptured some fifty miles to the south by the Middle Rio Grande Irrigation District.

Grandpa served as mayordomo several times. It was an elective office, chosen from among their number by the *parciantes*, all those individuals who held water rights. Although vested with authority by the irrigation district, which was overseen by elected commissioners, the mayordomo's authority was principally a moral one, validated by tradition.

Acequias are the arterial system of Hispano village life. They run through every community and by means of feeder ditches reach into every patch of cultivable land. Homes, fields, and pastures are laid out to permit access to water carried in those ditches. They were the first public works project of the Spanish-Mexican settlers of New Mexico, says my friend José Rivera, author of *Acequia Culture*. Even before they built the church, the settlers laid out the community's acequias in order to assure its material well-being.

In cattle culture, rustling was considered a crime, punishable by death, and punishment was frequently meted out summarily. In acequia culture, stealing water was a sin. The violator was subject to fines and, more important, to being reproved and therefore shamed. When Grandpa caught someone stealing water he sealed off the diversion, then stood at the sluice gate waiting for the guilty party to notice that the water had tailed off. The culprits, who were siphoning off what they deemed a tiny amount of water, usually spotted him on arrival and retreated indoors or deep into their lots. He confronted them only if they kept repeating the offense, in which case he walked up to the front door of the farmhouse and knocked loudly; if there was no response, he walked around to the kitchen door. There he usually met the woman of the house, who claimed not to know where the man of the house was and to have no knowledge of the water siphoning. In most cases, since it was during the day and men tended to be at work, a woman was diverting water to feed her flower garden or her chile patch. Grandpa let the violator off with a stern warning and moved on.

Water thievery during daylight hours was inconsequential, if irritating to the mayordomo, since it involved minute amounts of water. Multiple instances of theft did, of course, reduce the amount available to the assignee. More serious were the nocturnal diversions, which tended to be large scale. My grandfather left these to the assignee, who had to trek upstream to find out where the diversion had occurred, to resolve. Formal complaints came first to the mayordomo and then to the ditch commissioners for adjudication. Grandpa was called to testify in those hearings, to confirm that he had assigned the water to the complainant and to respond to questions about the offender's history with the acequia. These usually resulted in a fine and sometimes in the denial of water to the offender for a restricted period.

The thefts occasionally resulted in altercations. Dad, an avid reader of the *Rio Grande Sun*, loved to read about the incidents to whoever would listen: "So and So of Lower San Pedro Road was charged by Such and Such with assault stemming from the diversion of water from the Ciruelas ditch. The case will be heard by Justice of the Peace John Doe on Thursday." He particularly relished them if he knew one or more of the parties.

Foremost among the mayordomo's responsibilities was the annual ditch clearing. Each *parciante* was responsible for participating or for providing a hired hand to help. Clearing a ditch was a multiple-day, physically demanding task. It involved removing the sand and silt that built up on the streambed, cutting back the growth that encroached on the banks, removing the detritus that accumulated over the year, and repairing breaks caused by spring runoffs or gophers. My participation was limited to bringing water and lunch to Grandpa if the cleanup occurred when I was helping on the farm, but I liked to watch and sometimes to join in.

Ditch clearing was a mostly good-natured community affair, but the young men assigned to meet familial obligations or the hired hands sometimes failed to pull their weight, left early, or complained incessantly about the task. Grandpa had no patience with malingerers or whiners. He shamed the family members and fired the hired hands, sometimes incurring the responsible *parciante*'s wrath. But his word was law, and the respect he was held in kept the complainants in check.

Central to the acequia's institution in New Mexico is the blessing of the waters and the fields. It takes place on May 15, the day set aside for the patron saint of farmers, San Isidro Labrador. Many, if not most, Hispano communities celebrate July 25, the feast day of Saint James. Santiago Matamoros, as the warrior saint is known, was the patron saint of the military forces that led advances into the various parts of the New World. His supposed interventions on behalf of Hispano villagers in their conflicts with Apaches, Comanches, Kiowas, Navajos, and Utes assured Santiago of his standing in the Hispano world. But more in tune with their daily realities is the saintly gentleman farmer, San Isidro, a favorite subject of Hispano woodcarvers and painters.

The parishioners of Capilla de San Pedro did not honor the tradition for some reason. I like to think that if they had, Grandpa would have been present, if at a distance, hat in hand, as the priest blessed the field and the water flowed along the Ciruelas ditch. He may have been a *protestante*, but he was also a member of the community and, of course, the mayordomo.

† † † "*Voulez vous?*" and "*forchette,*" Tío Pedro answers when I ask what he remembers about being in France. The sexual innuendo in the former escapes me, but the latter sounds suspicious. His demeanor and the movement of his eyes contribute to his reputation for being a rascal. Pedro Barela, my grandfather's brother, is a stout man, fair of skin, with gray-green eyes. Unlike Grandpa, Tío Pedro got drafted during World War I and ended up in France just before the war ended. World War II was part of my personal experience, even though I was born in 1939, but World War I was exotic, and I wanted to know what it was like for him. During the day he is caught up helping Grandpa with chores, but after dinner, when we are sitting around the table, he responds to my questions.

The Barelas were not a major presence in my life in the way that the Tafoyas, my grandmother's family, were. Grandpa's family was a mystery to me, and Tío Pedro represented an opportunity to learn about it. But around Grandma he was very discreet and I was unable to get much out of him. What I had figured out, however, was that Grandpa's relations were not *protestantes.*

Tío Pedro made the trip down the mountain from Las Truchas alone. To my knowledge neither his wife nor his daughter ever accompanied him. I don't know whether he came to visit or whether Grandpa sought his help—probably a bit of both. Tío Pedro clearly enjoyed his brother's company, and he returned home with money in his pocket and produce in the back of the truck. Grandpa always needed help on the farm, especially after Ray left, Ernesto passed away, and Viola married. Aurora was Grandpa's all-purpose hand, but school took priority and some of the chores required greater strength than she had. Though slow, Tío Pedro moved bales of hay, crates of fruit, and farm equipment with ease. On occasion our visits coincided. After dinner, as we sat around the table removing pebbles and other foreign matter from the dried beans or peas Grandpa had bought or traded for, he told stories and posed riddles for our entertainment. His humor was infectious, and even Grandma, whose usual mode was disapproval, smiled and laughed at his stories.

Only one other of Grandfather's brothers visited the farm, though he was not, I sensed, a welcome guest. Tío Epifanio was received in the small *portal* that sheltered the entrances to the two formal rooms of the farmhouse. On his rare visits Grandma pulled two chairs out of the kitchen and into the portal, one for Tío Epifanio and one for Grandpa. She then retreated into the house, emerging only when Grandpa called out that Epifanio was leaving. When I asked about her obvious lack of hospitality she only wrinkled her nose, avoiding any further response by asking me to fetch something. I came to understand that Grandma associated Catholics with liquor and preferred that neither enter her home. Epifanio apparently represented both, or so Mom suggested. Viola, on the other hand, who liked any kind of company and all kinds of stories, had a more interesting and titillating explanation. Tío Epifanio had stolen Primo Isidoro's wife, Lola, and left him to bring up their baby, Emilia, who was Viola's age and with whom she was close. Grandma strongly disapproved of Epifanio, but he was Grandpa's brother and thus had to be received.

The only other Barelas Grandma received warmly were Tía Leonardita, the widow of Grandpa's youngest brother, also named Isidoro, and her children. My grandparents were very close to and very protective of her. Her husband died in their home a few weeks before Cousin Hope and I were born, on his way back to Las Truchas, having taken ill while working in Wyoming. Tía helped out during the harvest and tended to Grandma and Ernesto whenever they took ill. Fidencia, her oldest daughter, continued in her footsteps, helping Mom with my brother Ibáñez when he was injured and attending to her when she became ill with cancer.

The principal Barela connection after both Pedro and Epifanio passed away continued to be Tía Leonardita and two of her four children, Susie and Hope, who lived with her. Tía's house was across the plaza from the Catholic church.

Like the rest of the Barela family, Leonardita was Catholic, but Susie worked at the Presbyterian mission and Hope, just a few days younger than me, was enrolled at the mission school.

The summer after I turned twelve I accompanied Grandpa on a visit to his mother, Refugio Fernández, at her home in Las Truchas. Her small adobe house, which sat across the lane from the Catholic church, was lit only by a kerosene lamp. Great-grandmother Refugio was blind, but the lamp provided illumination for her companion, whom we knew as Mana Trinidad. Grandpa brought them produce from the farm, as well as coffee, bread, sugar, and salt he bought at the Tafoya General Store in Las Truchas, all of which Great-grandmother Refugio stowed in an ancient wooden chest. Rummaging through the chest, she found a package of equally ancient cookies, which she served along with reheated coffee. She sat at the kitchen table and felt around the table until she located her bag of Bull Durham tobacco and leaves, then rolled herself a cigarette. Mana Trinidad did not smoke, but I noticed a tobacco stamp on the left side of her forehead. It was, Mom explained, a folk remedy against headaches. Sitting at the table, their weathered faces illuminated by the light from the kerosene lamp, the two incarnated the wizened women that populated the fables and tales of my storybooks. I do not recall ever seeing Refugio Fernández before or after, nor do I remember attending her funeral, although she died in 1952, when I was thirteen years old and quite aware of deaths.

As we headed home, I asked Grandpa whether he had known his grandfather. "*Sí*," he responded. He was helping his father repair a fence, he told me, and as they were working he asked him who his father was. José de la Luz, his father, pointed with his chin to a man on a horse making his way down the lane, waving a gun, barely able to remain astride, and said: "*¿Ves ese hombre, el del gorrito y la chamarra azul? Ese señor, Desiderio Barela, ese es mi papá.*" His grandfather Desiderio, Grandpa told me, was a Civil War veteran and had fought at the battle of Valverde in southern New Mexico. He continued to wear his Union blue and was wont to parade the narrow road that ran through Truchas and up to the Barela holdings at the base of the Truchas Peaks. In the course of my explorations, I found my great-great-grandfather Desiderio Barela listed on the rolls of the New Mexico Volunteers, led into the battle by Kit Carson. The Union force, composed mainly of inexperienced, untrained, and badly equipped men like Desiderio, fled the scene of battle at their first encounter, routed by a superior Confederate force.

Tepid archival researcher that I am, my efforts to uncover the Barela patrilineal line ended with José Antonio Barela, father to José Antonio Barela and grandfather to José Desiderio Barela. Cousin Susie Barela, who became the matriarch Tía Leonardita had been, came to my rescue. A distant relation had put together their genealogy, tracing the line all the way back to one of the brothers Barela-Jaramillo, who accompanied the *adelantado* Juan de Oñate in the 1598 *entrada*. Like my Madrid ancestors, the Barelas made their way back north after being expelled in the Pueblo Revolt of 1680. Comparison of Hispano family trees reveals multiple common ancestors and unsurprising coincidences. My maternal ancestor Cristóbal Barela's son contracted for marriage with my paternal ancestor Francisco Madrid's daughter, Lucía. Roque Madrid, son of the field marshal, was a *vecino* of Quemado, subsequently known as Córdova, along with José Antonio Barela, the father.

The history of Hispanos, particularly residents of the Rio Arriba, is one of propinquity and consanguinity. For two centuries Hispanos lived cheek by jowl in the reduced spaces of the Rio Grande Valley and its tributary river valleys. In a world of limited options, one cozied up to one's relations. "*A la prima se le arrima*," cracked the young men of my generation, when warned that an attractive young woman who had caught their eye was a family relation, if somewhat removed. Small wonder that the church was so concerned with marriage bans. In the end, we Hispanos are all intimately related.

MARCHANTE

† † † Only a few *recuerdos* remain from my grandparents' farm in San Pedro: Navajo and Rio Grande serapes, two benches that served as seats at the kitchen table, three copper vats for reducing fat and processing corn, two branding irons, a brass ladle for scooping grain and meal out of storage containers, the wooden paddle Grandma Barela used to pull bread from the adobe oven, and several tattered record books. Some are accounts of my grandfather's water assignments; the most interesting ones are the records of transactions with his clients.

Over four decades, my grandfather peddled the produce he and my grandmother grew throughout the communities of the Rio Arriba. Before I was born he was providing fresh produce and dried corn and chile products to miners in Madrid and Cerrillos, accepting company scrip in exchange. For many years he traveled to the Jicarilla Apache Reservation to sell his goods during their annual feast day in September, returning with jewelry and rugs for which he bartered. I came to know the plazas of the upper Rio Chama Valley, where I grew up, principally in his company, but I also ranged farther afield with him, to places I would not otherwise have come to know, including the mining communities of Madrid and Cerrillos, already semideserted when I visited them.

In journals similar to the ones in my possession Grandpa recorded his commercial transactions and made notes about promises, agreements, and requests involving his customers. The records had to do with credit he extended to his customers, but they also provide a listing of the produce he sold and bartered: Doña Rosa owed him $2 for apples. Don Filigonio purchased one sack of green chile and owed $3. Don Santiago paid $2 on his account. Doña Estefanitas owed $5 on her purchase of blue cornmeal, posole, and ground red chile. Esquipula Sanchez owed $1.50 on a crate of tomatoes. Much of his trade involved barter—a load of firewood, a side of beef, a sack of pinto beans, twenty pounds of dried peas, a lamb or a kid, several cowhides. He listed the cash value of the bartered items and maintained a running tally of the produce taken in exchange.

By age ten I was accompanying him on selling trips to the villages around Tierra Amarilla. Our arrival at one of the many plazas where his customers lived triggered great excitement among children, particularly once fruit was in season. Some ran alongside the truck while others scurried to their respective homes crying out, "*Marchante, marchante. Aquí llegó el marchante.*" Grandpa, known to his clients as Mano Ramos, hopped out of the cab and swung himself up to the truck bed. I scrambled up behind as the kids from the surrounding houses began to gather. My job was to keep watch on the produce while he was occupied with his clients, since both children and adults could slip their hands through the slats of the truck's platform and help themselves.

The women issued forth slowly from the houses, drying their hands on the apron tied around their waist. Grandpa greeted them one and all: "*Buenos días le de Dios. ¿Cómo le va, marchanta?*" Then he listed his cargo for them. On occasion, depending on the hour, the man of the house also emerged, rolling down his shirtsleeves. Many were away, tending sheep in the pastures of Wyoming and Montana. He greeted them with the same term they used with him, *marchante*, and recited his offerings to them as well. But he knew who did the buying. Turning to the women, he asked what appealed to them: "*¿Qué se le ofrece, marchanta?*"

The term intrigued me. I loved to hear it spoken: *marchante*, *marchanta.* Grandpa was the *marchante*, but his

clients were also *marchantes*. I wondered why it applied to both seller and customer. And unlike *protestante* and other similar forms I subsequently learned, *comerciante*, *parciante*, it took on a gendered form. Years later, while I was doing doctoral studies in Spanish, I learned of its ancient origins and uses in a class on historical linguistics. The word is of Latin origin and comes to both Spanish and English through French. In its original meaning it refers simply to a merchant. In the Spanish of the Americas, however, it designates the buyer's preferences, and in Mexico it marks the preferred seller. As used in New Mexico and in my grandfather's case, he was their preferred merchant, and they were his preferred customers.

Grandpa started his rounds in late spring, as soon as the country lanes had dried enough to permit him to wander off the asphalt and gravel roads. The bulk of his sales were the staples of the Hispano diet: posole and *chicos*, dried corn used for pork-based hominy soups, dried *chile colorado* in both ground and pod form, and *harina de maíz azul*, a finely ground meal made of toasted blue corn and used to make a soothing porridge, *atole*, a comfort food of pre-Hispanic origins prized by the elderly, who assigned it therapeutic properties. These products show up on his records year-round and were the principal source of his earnings. He closed out the year in November as he began it in May, selling apples, dried fruit, dried corn products, and dried chile. The remainder of the sales he recorded reflected the growing season. In June, after he had completed spring planting, he supplemented his merchandise with scallions, radishes, carrots, and lettuce, as well as tomatoes jumpstarted in my grandmother's makeshift nursery. Cherries, an early July crop, were followed by apricots and plums, then peaches, and subsequently pears. The bounty mounted over the summer as tomatoes, corn, onions, cabbage, and string beans came into fruition. The crops most desired by his customers, *chile verde* and melons, were available late August. Grandpa planted chile, cantaloupe, honeydews, and watermelons in stages over the spring and early summer to make them available from late summer into early fall. Apples, the main fruit crop, were an anomaly, since early varieties were available in July, long before the highly desired Delicious were ready for market. September brought Jonathan and Golden Delicious, as well as pears, which were supplemented in October by Red Delicious, Winesaps, Stamens, and McIntoshes.

When there were multiple clients at hand, he had me attend to the transaction if it was a simple cash one. I measured out cherries, plums, apricots, apples, tomatoes, and green chile pods in containers that had previously contained five and ten pounds of lard. Grandpa was responsible for larger amounts—a crate of tomatoes, a bushel of peaches, or a sack of green chile—and, of course, he handled all credit arrangements. Dried goods were sold by weight, measured on a small scale and ladled into small paper bags from recycled flour sacks or large tin containers. These were placed against the cab, covered with a tarp, and exposed only to extract foodstuffs.

Once my legs were long enough to reach the pedals and after Grandpa had dispatched his centrally located clients, he had me chug along the road in first gear while he walked from house to house announcing his wares. When he got a response, he signaled me to stop. I slipped the gearshift into neutral, and if he returned to the truck with a client in tow I turned off the motor and set the emergency brake. Then I climbed up to the truck bed and watched as he conducted business. When the transaction was complete, we moved on to the next set of houses.

I loved to go along, since during the school year it freed me from weekend chores and during the summer months it relieved the tedium of staying at home. Moreover, in the evening when he was counting up his money he would pay me a dollar for my labors. A dollar was a good amount in the late 1940s, enough to purchase ten cokes, ten Hershey bars, or ten comic books.

DON RAMOS

† † † The farm was not my favorite place when I was an adolescent or a teenager. But when I was a child it was wondrous—twelve acres to roam; multiple buildings and structures to explore; chickens, rabbits, pigs, cows, and occasionally sheep, goats, and horses to chase. As was the case with my father's family, I was the first Barela grandchild and similarly doted upon. Mother's two brothers, Ernesto and Ramos Jr., were adolescents when I was born, and her sister Viola was nine. Aurora, only five years my senior, became more of a sibling than an aunt. They were all disposed to indulge me. I tagged along behind them as they carried out their chores, and when I became hot, tired, or bored I headed for the cool recesses of the farmhouse.

Once I could distinguish between a weed and a plant, however, I joined my grandfather's workforce. I spent part or most of my summers between the ages of ten and seventeen on the farm. Whether it was because my grandparents asked for me to come or because my parents didn't want three kids making demands on them, I was sent downriver as soon as school was out. Ernesto died when I was eleven, Viola married when I was twelve, and Aurora left when I was thirteen. By then I was a full-fledged worker. I didn't like the heat or the repetitive, backbreaking nature of row-crop work, but I particularly abhorred not having playmates and friends.

During the day I was out with Grandpa, who stopped only for lunch and a midday nap, slowing down only after supper. We did the demanding tasks—plowing, harrowing, planting, weeding, mowing, butchering, and harvesting—early in the morning. Midmorning I accompanied him as he checked on fences and ditches. In the heat of the afternoon we attended to farm equipment, sorted out containers, and sharpened farm implements in the shade of the cottonwoods. Then we returned to the heavy chores, though at a slower pace.

Despite the heat, the drudgery, and the lack of companionship, there were benefits to being on the farm. Grandpa occasionally treated me to a coke and candy while we were on our rounds, and he would slip me a couple of dollars from time to time. Best of all, long before I was eligible to drive on public roads I was steering the pumper truck down the orchard rows while Grandpa sprayed the fruit trees. By age twelve I was driving the tractor, happily turning over soil, mowing alfalfa, and weeding row crops in their early stages. When Grandpa took me with him to peddle his wares I got to drive the farm truck. My grandparents gave me much more leeway than my parents did, and once I had my driver's license I had the run of the immediate area.

Although my grandmother Trinidad loved me, what I wanted was my grandfather Ramos's attention and favor. As the first grandchild I initially had both, but Grandpa had his favorites. He much preferred my younger brother Ibáñez. But I was family—a much-needed pair of hands—and he treated me well, if sometimes gruffly.

While not unkind or cruel, my grandfather was neither sensitive nor gentle. He undoubtedly had a rough, peasant upbringing; farm life was brutal. He was not used to coddling animals, equipment, or people. Cows, pigs, and horses were all subject to being kicked or cuffed, as were his children. I witnessed him launch quick kicks at Aurora and Ernesto when he became displeased with them. On one occasion Grandma came rushing out of the kitchen to intervene, because Ernesto, who was a large man, had decided to retaliate in kind, and matters were getting out of hand.

I never experienced my grandfather's physical wrath, but

he was exceedingly demanding and impatient. There was work to be done, and it needed to be done now. When I didn't heave to immediately, he called me a *huevón*, a lazy bum. His ultimate *maldición*, spat out when I botched a task, also involved my testicles: *Malhaya tus huevos.* Since at that age I had no idea what purpose they served, damning them made no impression. I was more affected by my grandfather's tone. But I knew my grandmother would be sympathetic and that I was under her protection.

As creatures tied to the soil, my grandparents were understandably focused on the ground. I came to appreciate that my grandmother's downcast eyes also reflected her emotional state. For Grandpa, keeping his eyes cast down was essential to his daily existence: he had to survey his crops, check on his ditches, and tend his livestock. He raised his gaze only when he addressed us or when he engaged in conversation with relatives and clients. Many years later my professional life took me to the Midwest, where I was exposed to corporate-scale agriculture. It occurred to me then that Grandpa would have done well at farming on a large scale. He loved equipment, was always acquiring the latest implements, and, much to my grandmother's dismay, was forever renting plots of land to plant additional crops. I came to appreciate that he especially loved engaging with people, whether the *quejantes* who appeared before him when he was a justice, the *parciantes* who solicited water from him, or the *marchantes* who purchased his goods. Whether his gregariousness was genetic or cultivated, I ended up inheriting it. And like him, I have spent my life attending to duties and responsibilities and taking on more than I should.

My appreciation for my grandfather Ramos grew over time. A literate and intelligent man, he studied and practiced the law in Spanish, kept informed about the world through *El nuevo mexicano*, and, like Grandma, read the Bible faithfully. Despite his patriarchal character, he encouraged and supported his daughters' aspirations. He neither spoke nor read English well, yet he ably navigated the commercial, judicial, and political English-speaking world. A

Hispano in an Anglo world and a *protestante* in a Catholic environment, he negotiated both spaces with assurance. He was trusting in his dealings. He might get scammed once but never twice. "*Contigo no pierdo*," he would tell persons who made a personal request of him or bought something on credit. I have made it my own, assuring friends and colleagues that I stand only to gain from my investment in them.

Given our itinerant existence, the farm became home for my parents, my siblings, and my own children. When my grandfather grew too old to sustain it, my parents purchased it from him. He divided his remaining years between the farm and his daughter Viola's home in Utah. I returned again and again, until there was no farm to return to. Surrounded as it was by lands held by Santa Clara Pueblo, whose leaders had learned history's lessons and held close access to and through them, the erstwhile "city" of Española exercised the law of eminent domain to expropriate the farm from my parents in order to build a bridge across the Rio Grande and expand its sewage facilities. A plant that cleans wastes previously stored in septic tanks or leaked into the Rio Grande sits on five of the original acres. An animal shelter occupies the space where the farmhouse and storage rooms stood. The remaining acres lie fallow. Only the stump of an ancient cottonwood remains as testimony to the island of *protestantes*.

LAS ORILLAS DEL MUNDO

† † † I grew up at *las orillas del mundo*, a place known to my eighteenth-century ancestors as the edge of the world, in a river valley located at the rim of the Colorado Plateau and the foot of the Colorado Rockies, on the ancestral hunting grounds of Utes and Navajos, at the heart of a community land grant settled in the period before the United States occupied the area and created the Territory of New Mexico. For several decades, the area I still call home was contested territory, subject to raids carried out by Navajos and Utes. Subse-

quently it became contested property, claimed by the heirs to the Tierra Amarilla Land Grant of 1841 but held by absentee land companies and the U.S. Forest Service. The boundaries of the land grant that led to the area's settlement area consisted of the horizon, whatever the compass point. In the valley of my youth the physical horizons seemed to extend forever. But the social horizons were limited, and the social divisions—class, ethnic, religious—were as sharply defined as the topographical ones were at the sunset hour.

Tierra Amarilla was the seat of county government, and as a consequence it acquired the accoutrements of a small commercial center: multiple grocery stores, gas stations, auto repair shops and saloons, a movie theater, a barbershop, and a high school. My world consisted of our family home, the courthouse where my mother served as a public official, and the public school my father directed. My earliest memories are of looking out the windows of my parents' home, which was less than twenty-five miles from the Colorado border. Highway 84, then a gravel road, ran through Tierra Amarilla and in front of our home. In winter the ground was blanketed with snow, but from late spring through early fall the yard was covered with weeds, including edible greens—*quelites*, lamb's quarters, and *verdolagas*, purslane. When the wind blew it exposed the silvery undersides of the *quelites*, but it was the pulpy strands of *verdolagas* I most liked to step on and pick and squeeze. *Cizañas*, Russian thistle, grew at the base of the woven wire fence surrounding the yard, from seeds deposited by tumbleweeds trapped by the fence. Prickly stalks of hollyhocks lined the house, and as they flowered their weight caused them to tilt away from the wall. I love the English name as much as I do the Spanish—*varas de San José*, Saint Joseph's staff. The ubiquitous and hardy *rosa de Castilla* hugged the front porch, and a stunted lilac bush grew in the corner of the yard. Across the road sat an adobe house with a flat roof, where my playmate Leo lived.

From my vantage point I could keep track of my *paisanos*' comings and go-

ings: Doña Rosaura, Leo's mother, hanging out her wash or sprinkling the yard to keep down the dust; Abrán, Leo's brother, at the woodpile chopping wood and, in winter, clearing snow off their roof; Don Lionel, who delivered the mail to nearby towns on his daily rounds, via sulky in summer and sleigh in winter; my parents' friend and frequent visitor, Melchor Tafoya, the county sheriff, who honked and waved to me as he headed north to deliver summons; the bus that brought passengers and the mail upcountry daily except Sunday; the Charles Ilfeld truck that delivered merchandise weekly to stores throughout the upper Rio Chama watershed. *Ancianos*, stooped with age, on their way to catch up on gossip at the courthouse; an occasional horseman coming into town to carry out a chore; older kids heading to or from school or on an errand. I was always on the lookout for Dulcinea, who babysat me evenings and weekends, and I called out to her when she walked by. She could not hear me, but she always looked for me and waved when she saw me.

My favorite sight was flocks of sheep being driven to pasture in the spring or to market in the fall. They clogged the highway. The occasional motorists honked their horns and called out to the sheepherders, but they paid no mind. My dog Brownie, an elegant Springer spaniel, ran along the woven wire fence surrounding our yard, desperate to get out and nip at their hindquarters. The sheep ignored him, and the sheepdogs paused only to mark the fence posts. The shepherds wore *pecheras*, bib overalls, and walked behind the flock, whistling at the sheepdogs. The supply wagon followed, drawn by a team of horses. In spring it was full of *pencos*, the orphaned lambs. Occasionally I spotted a rare black one.

For the annual fiestas, July 24 and 25, when New Mexico's patron saints, Santiago and Santa Ana, are honored, wagons rolled into town in the days preceding the festivities. Some came from as far as the Jicarilla Apache Reservation, a two-day trip by wagon to the northwest. Others originated in the *placitas* of the upper Rio Chama watershed. Bedding, firewood, and cookware hung from the sides of the wagon beds. Colts were tethered to some of the wagons. Their mothers, in harness and drawing the wagons, turned their heads anxiously when they whinnied. Dogs trotted alongside, provoking a ferocious response from the local canines, which ranted at them from the safety of fenced yards. The Apache families camped on the floodplain next to the river. The Hispano families sought out the yards of friends and relatives or pulled their wagons into Big Six's compound behind Lito's Restaurant, Ballroom, and Bar.

The women, babies, and girls rode on wooden chests and benches covered with blankets in the wagon bed and looked out the back. Lambs and kids, destined to be slaughtered and cooked during the stay, occupied the wagon bed as well. The men rode up front or accompanied the wagon on horseback, and the younger boys rode with their elders in the buckboard seat. Young or old, all wore hats with high crowns. The Apaches' hats, uniformly black, were adorned with silver and sometimes beaded bands. The Apaches, males and female alike, sported festive shirts and blouses of mustard yellow, electric blue,

carmine red. The older Hispano males wore drab wool suits, the younger ones jeans and khaki shirts. The women draped elegant but subdued shawls over their shoulders—except for the widows, who dressed in black. All wore bonnets, even the little girls.

My maternal grandfather, Ramos Barela, came into town during the feast days, his truck loaded with fresh produce and dried corn and chile products, which along with beans constituted the staples of the Hispano and Apache diets during the winter months. He claimed a space across the road in front of Lito's and set up a canvas tarp to provide shade for his cargo and himself. The far left side of the window permitted me a view of the parked wagons, cars, and trucks and the people walking up and down the road that ran through town. Even inside I could hear the din from establishments, the car horns, shouts, and music.

At night, music and shouts emanating from Lito's, floating above the roar of his electric generator, penetrated our living room. Lito and his rival Félix

Esquibel, owner of the Green Leaf Café and Bar, both had generators and thus could stay open past dusk. We also had one, as did our neighbor across the lane, Don Victoriano Ulibarrí. My father powered it up on weekday evenings when we had company and on weekends. Otherwise our lighting consisted of a Coleman lantern in the room we were occupying and kerosene lamps in the rest of the house.

The scene before me was usually the more tranquil one of people going about their daily business. I stood at the window and waited for Leo to come over to play, or for my parents to come home for lunch. The sun warmed the windowsill in the morning. My favorite toys were under the dining room table, where I retreated if there were nothing of interest outside my window. I didn't have far to go to get my bottle or a snack. My blanket was draped on a chair behind me. This area and the living room couch were my *querencias*, the secure spaces I sought out when my parents were away. As the morning progressed, I felt heat emanating from the stove in the kitchen behind me.

I have lost the memory, if I ever had one, of the house's interior, but not of the changing quality of the light as the day progressed: the crisp light of my early morning vigil at the window, the diffused gentle light of my midmorning snack in the kitchen, the hushed soft light of my afternoon nap on the living room couch, the rays of the setting sun cutting through the drapes as I sat on my father's lap, the warm glow of kerosene lamps my mother lit at dusk, the incandescence of the Coleman lamp as we sat around the table at night.

My memory calls up the aromas—beans cooking, chiles roasting, meat frying—that wafted through the house and intermingled with familiar domestic sounds: the crackle of piñon wood burning in the kitchen stove; the poker screeching on the stove lid; the ringing of the bean pot lid; the rumble of the rolling pin on tortilla dough; the pat of tortillas being turned on the griddle; and the singing and humming of our housekeeper, who doubled as my nanny, as she went about her chores.

The snapshots of my childhood confirm some of my memories. Our house sits on an elevated foundation and has stairs leading up to a small, stuccoed porch. The dining room faces east and occupies the northeast corner of the house. One snapshot shows me peeking out of the window. Another has me among the hollyhocks, looking guilty; I have been eating dirt. My favorite shows me in bib overalls, seated in my pedal car. Brownie is at my side. The yard is overgrown with weeds, and the hollyhocks behind me are leafy and stunted. Another photo poses me with my sister and brother. Concha is still a baby but sits upright in her cradle. We are both looking at the camera. My brother Ibáñez, however, is distracted by something outside the frame. My mother claimed it was a flock of sheep passing by, but Nene, as he was known, could be distracted by almost anything. Still another photo shows me with my right arm outstretched in greeting. My father smiled whenever he saw it. His friends, he told me, teased him, asking if I was practicing to join the Hitler Youth.

EL NUEVO RORRO

† † † The earliest snapshot taken of me shows me sitting in a dishpan, naked except for a straw hat with cotton bolos hanging from its brim. It is the first of two baby pictures that feature me in the nude. Both are discreet. The second, a studio portrait, has me perched on a settee, looking very alert. They would have been taken in my first year of life. I was born at the end of the Great Depression and on the cusp of World War II. Home was the "cabin" my mother had rented during her stint as deputy county clerk before being elected the chief officer. It was one of three two-room dwellings across the irrigation ditch from the courthouse and opposite Charlie Farrell's gas station and grocery store. By 1940 we occupied a home north of the courthouse. Later snapshots pose me in front of the latter dwelling.

I was known to one and all as Rorro, so named because my father's friends in Los Lunas would inquire about *el nuevo rorro*, the recently arrived baby, on his return from a weekend visit to us in Tierra Amarilla. And thus Rorro I became, still called that seven decades later, affectionately if sheepishly by my aunts and uncles and aggressively by my younger cousins. I may have traveled far and done much, but those cousins have need to remind me that I am still Rorro to them. My contemporaries, when we chance to meet, recall that my brother and I were known widely as Rorro Nene Supper, so dubbed because of my father's habit of standing on the front porch and calling us home for dinner.

I became a courthouse denizen soon after I was born. At first my nanny would take me to my mother's office several times a day to be nursed. Subsequently I was fetched from home whenever my mother's constituents asked after *el rorro*. Inevitably a clerk carried me off to one of the other offices. When I was not returned or when my nanny could not find me, my mother had to go from office to office looking for me amid the giggles of the clerks, who had made a game of "stealing" me. By age two, Mom said, I had become a willing conspirator, disposed to hide in vaults and cabinets and under desks. My rewards, besides attention, were cokes and chocolate, both of which were at a premium during the war. One early snapshot, which I can no longer locate, betrays me. I have a ring of chocolate around my mouth.

As I grew older, I had the run of the courthouse on my own. My two favorite places were the courtroom on the second floor, which the janitor would let me into, and the jail in the basement, which I could only enter in the company of the jailor. In the courtroom I could pretend to my heart's content: declaim to the jury, interrogate witnesses, demand order in the court, pronounce judgment on the accused. Mostly, however, I spun myself on the judge's swivel chair or slid on the jury benches. The jail was a different matter. Dimly lit and musty smelling like my grandparents' cellar, it both attracted and scared me. Descending into it was an adventure. I imagined it as Daniel's dungeon, from my biblical storybook. The inmates did not scare me. I knew them and they knew me, since some were trustees who carried water or chopped wood for us. But there was always the thought that I would end up locked in one of the cells by accident, in the dark, surrounded by who knows what creatures lurking in the corners and under the cot. And Simón Martínez, the jailor and our neighbor, was always threatening to toss kids who misbehaved in jail, under lock and key. My visits were thus quick ones, and I always left with my heart in my throat.

Quite apart from attention, cokes, and chocolate, the courthouse gave me, quite literally, a bigger window on the world. Its windows were wide and high, and the walls were so thick I was able to sit on the windowsills comfortably. From there I monitored the upper Rio Chama watershed: the plume of water that plunged down the rock face of the Brazos Peaks in late spring; the blooming of lilacs, roses, and hollyhocks over the spring and summer; the changes in the coloration of the aspen groves and scrub oak patches as fall made its way down the mountainsides; the first appearance of snow on the crests of the mountains across the Colorado border.

The most interesting view, however, was the traffic coming into town from the south and pulling up in front of Charlie Farrell's gas station. Most of the vehicles belonged to local ranchers or persons from around the county who had business in the county seat, but others—newer, larger, fancier ones—bore Texas plates. Their owners came to fish and cool off in resorts on the upper reaches of the Rio Chama watershed or the Conejos River Valley of southern Colorado located over the Cumbres Pass to the north, in places with storybook names: Menkhaven, Rainbow Lodge, Elkhorn Ranch. I knew from poring over news magazines and listening to the radio that a world different from and larger than mine existed. The parameters of my experience extended, to be sure, as far as the metropolises of Santa Fe and Las Vegas. But the occupants of these vehicles were different from my *paisanos* and even from the *americanos* who lived among us—the Farrell family; the Wisdoms, who ran the fish hatchery; Butch Long, the majordomo of the T. D. Burns estate, and his family; and the various ranchers and resort owners. Moreover, unlike their transient migrant brethren—wildcatters, roughnecks, and loggers who arrived in late spring and left in late fall—the summer visitors were tall, healthy-looking, affluent, self-assured, and assertive. They stopped at Charlie Farrell's to replenish ice chests, check tire pressure and oil levels, clean windshields, and gas up. The men exited from their large and luxurious cars to oversee the services; the women rarely did, except to use the restroom. Having determined that the facilities consisted of a unisex outhouse, they postponed the call of nature or, if the call was urgent, wandered over to use the courthouse facilities.

But the usual fare on my daily visual menu were my *paisanos*, who came into town on foot or on horseback, in wagons, by truck or car, occasionally via the daily bus, to buy groceries, retrieve mail, or conduct business at the courthouse. I followed their trajectory from the southeast corner of the elevated first floor. They dismounted and tethered their horses or parked their vehicles and got out. After stretching and consulting with each other, they proceeded in separate directions or together to the courthouse, the various commercial establishments, or the post office.

Most came by the county clerk's office to say hello at some point, even if they didn't have business there. Unlike the offices of the county assessor, treasurer, or sheriff, which people visited principally out of necessity and which frequently involved some unpleasant obligation or messy problem, the county clerk's office was an unthreatening, uncomplicated space. Like her fellow elected officials, my mother always interrupted whatever she was doing to visit with her constituents. Unlike her fellow officials, she was female, young, pretty, bright, and vivacious. Mom spoke English and Spanish equally well and was at ease with both common folks and visiting dignitaries. She listened to their stories, laughed at their jokes, asked about family, and offered advice when asked. Always respectful, she greeted the elders as Don and Doña and used the polite *Usted* in her exchanges with them. Visiting officials were addressed as counselor, judge, governor, congressman, senator. She called only her staff and fellow elected officials by their first name, but in the latter case, if speaking to them in Spanish, she used the respectful form of address.

LA TIERRA AMARILLA

† † † As we leave the house, the extended Salazar family drives by. I wave at Dora, my classmate, who rides in the back of the truck. They are probably on their way to church for Saturday morning confession, since Father Austin will move on to other parishes later in the day. My mother and I are also on our way to church, in a manner of speaking. My grandfather, on his monthly trip to deliver produce to his *marchantes* in the upper Rio Chama watershed, has left fruit and vegetables for us before heading back to the family farm. We are driving to Chama to share the produce with the Presbyterian pastor and his spouse.

Earlier in the week, on our morning walk to school, Dora quizzed me once again about *protestantes*. Except for the Martínez family, which lives farther up the road, we are the only Hispano non-Catholics she knows. "If someone in your family dies," she asks, "where are you going to bury them? You know you *protestantes* can't be buried in the camposanto." She reminds me that when the Martínez's grandmother died last winter, they had to bury her on the hill behind the house. "*Allá en el chamizal*," she says, pointing with her chin. Out in the sagebrush-covered hills that surround my home community of Tierra Amarilla. "My uncle Eulogio," Dora recounts, "had to harness his team and hitch the sleigh to transport the corpse." I remember well. It was in January, just before my birthday. The ground was covered with snow and frozen solid.

Levi and his sons struggled for two days to dig the grave. Because of the bitter cold they hadn't been able to start their tractor.

I tell her I don't know. "Maybe in Chama, at the Protestant cemetery there," I say.

We drive past the courthouse and turn right in front of the T. D. Burns Jr. Mercantile Store and the adjacent post office. Don Felipe, the postmaster, looks up from his desk and waves. Don Adolfo is sitting in front of his movie house and nods as we go by. My friend Alfonsito is warming himself in the morning sun at the entrance to his father's gas station when we pull up. Alfonso Sr. comes out of the station and says, "Morning, Gaby." My mother is Gaby to her friends and colleagues. I have learned who doesn't know her well and tries to affect closeness, since to everyone else she is Mrs. Madrid.

They chat while Alfonsito gases us up and cleans our windshields. Then we drive west toward the canyon formed by the Chama River. To the north rise the Brazos Peaks, two ancient rounded elevations whose sheer rock faces resemble weathered corrugated roofing.

As we go past the camposanto, I ask my mother where she wants to be buried. "Why?" she asks, looking at me quizzically. I know my parents are concerned about the effects of growing up Protestant in a Roman Catholic environment. Earlier in the week she found a miracle medal I had snatched from my girlfriend in my jeans pocket. I explain. "Probably in Las Truchas, with the Tafoya clan, in the camposanto protestante," she says. We have only recently buried Tío Celso, Grandma Trinidad's brother, there. I recall the funeral procession winding its way down from the church to the cemetery. His sons, my mother's cousins, had cleared the hilltop where it sat of most of the native juniper and piñon trees, but the sagebrush proved resistant. Tío Celso's grave occupied a spot between two ancient *chamizos*. The cemetery had few graves. A barbed wire fence separated it from the new Roman Catholic cemetery, which had many more. A bulldozer had been brought in to clear the Catholic cemetery of sagebrush and scrub oak.

My mother slows at the lip of the canyon, where the highway curves down into the village of Los Ojos, on the banks of the Chama River. I can see La Puente to the south, and across the river La Plaza Blanca. As we wind down the side of the canyon I take note of the small crosses alongside the road. They mark *descansos*, places where funeral processions stopped to rest on the way to the cemetery. More recent ones, along the state highway and various county roads, memorialize victims of automobile accidents. We pass the grotto built into the cliff. It is dedicated to Our Lady of Lourdes, whose white alabaster statue faces north.

The Parkview Baptist Church and Medical Clinic are just past the irrigation ditch that runs along the edge of the canyon. On occasion we attend church there. It is a plain, elongated wooden building, without a bell tower. Only the small sign over the door marks its identity. Its untended yard is overgrown with weeds. Farther down the road, I look over my shoulder surreptitiously to see if I can catch a glimpse of my girlfriend. On a Saturday morning she will be helping

her mother do the wash. But only her younger brothers and the family's sheepdogs are in sight.

At Saint Joseph's Catholic Church we turn and head north along the ridge above the river. My mother asks me about my girlfriend. My siblings have already blabbed that I sat next to her at a football game. Someone at the courthouse has commented on how frequently the family car is seen in Los Ojos. "*Ya sabes que son muy católicos*," my mother says. I nod. My girlfriend's family are very devout Catholics, like most of their friends and neighbors. I quickly change the subject. Will we be going to the church on Sunday? For my parents, weekends are set aside for chores and relaxation, for dressing down. The local people do their weekly shopping, go to the movies and to dances, attend confession and mass. They tend to dress up. It embarrasses me to be seen in work clothes when my peers are in their finest.

Although the drive to Chama takes less than half an hour, the physical and human environments change over the fifteen-mile trip. Tierra Amarilla is situated on the north bank of Nutritas Creek, which flows west into the Chama River. Adobe houses with pitched tin roofs stand along the length of the elevated riverbank, on narrow, elongated strips of property. Narrow dirt lanes forking off from the main road lead to houses. Ivy and morning glories twine on the sloping portales that front them, and barrels at one end of the porch catch rainwater. Hollyhocks, lilac bushes, and the hardy roses with tiny blossoms known as *rosa de Castilla* grow around the covered water wells found in every yard. The main irrigation ditch, which follows the valley's contours, irrigates fields of corn, squash, peas, and fava beans. Sagebrush, scrub oak, juniper, and piñon trees grow on the adjacent foothills. Here and there, on an eroded ridge exposing the yellow clay soil that Tierra Amarilla takes its name from, is a solitary *pinavete*, a Ponderosa pine that somehow escaped being logged.

At the confluence of the Chama River and its principal tributary, the Brazos River, the highway angles north and west, into the adjacent foothills. The engine labors slightly with the change in elevation. The scrub oak is vibrant in shades of rust and gold. At the higher elevations groves of aspens, already a muted yellow, shimmer in the morning breeze. Despite the early morning chill, the sun has warmed the produce stowed in the backseat and the trunk. The scents are familiar ones—Delicious apples, Bartlett pears, and the last of the tomatoes, chiles, and honeydew melons.

A few miles later we reenter the Chama River Valley. Cabins constructed of shaved and varnished logs replace the adobe dwellings found downstream. Orange and yellow marigolds grow along the porches, and split-log fences mark the boundaries of grass-covered yards. The gravel lanes leading up to the houses are lined with aspens and firs. Discreet No Trespassing signs hang at the entrance to the driveways, and German shepherds and Doberman pinschers guard the approach to the homes. Taut wire fences strung on metal poles enclose the fields on both sides of the highway. On the forest side No Hunting signs are posted, and along the river they read No Fishing.

In its heyday Chama was a railhead for a narrow gauge railroad that transported ore, lumber, and sheep north to Denver and east to Wichita. The original settlement is reflected in the names on the older buildings: Foster's Hotel, Jones Mercantile Store, the Rainbow Theatre and Dance Hall, the Shamrock Bar. The town is situated at the northern end of an immense *merced*, the land grant known as La Tierra Amarilla, awarded by the Republic of Mexico to Manuel Martínez and various residents of Abiquiú in the 1830s.

The *merced* extended north to the southern Colorado Rockies and west to the mesas and canyons of the Colorado Plateau. A large part of the land grant passed into the hands of Thomas D. Catron, a member of the infamous Santa Fe Ring, and his cronies, including Thomas D. Burns, in the 1870s. Catron sold his portion ten years later to the Denver and Rio Grande Railroad Company, which laid out the town and stripped the surrounding forests. Burns kept his land. He sold timber and sheep to the railroad and dry goods to the locals at his mercantile stores, located in various plazas of the upper Rio Chama watershed.

No central plaza defines Chama. The town is laid out on a grid. Tourist lodges, cafes, and gas stations line the road leading into town, and modest frame houses stand on its residential streets. At the town's periphery the houses are mainly wooden shacks, unoccupied during the winter months. The main street, with its attendant commercial buildings, runs along the west bank of the river, overlooking the railroad yard. We drive by Wheeler's Electrical Supply Company, Harding's Drugstore, Kelly's Food Market, and the Chama office of Rio Arriba State Bank, owned by the Brasher family. On the northern end of the street are the prime residences—two-story dwellings covered with white clapboard and surrounded by white picket fences—and our destination, the Chama Valley Presbyterian Church.

We pull up at the manse, which is adjacent to the church. Behind a white picket fence is a nicely tended lawn. My parents are not members of this church, and we worship there only occasionally. We spend holidays with my maternal grandparents and accompany them to the Española Valley Evangelical United Brethren Church. When we visit my father's family, we attend services at the Spanish Presbyterian mission church in Old Town Las Vegas. During the winter months my parents sleep in while my siblings and I entertain ourselves. Summer Sundays are set aside for all-day fishing excursions.

The parishioners, local residents, own businesses or are professionals. My parents come in contact with them only occasionally, my mother in the course of her duties as a county official, my father in his capacity as principal of the Tierra Amarilla schools. We are the only Hispano worshippers. When we do attend, the parishioners greet us politely as we file out of church and go on their way. Once the congregation starts its exit, the pastor's wife slips quietly out the back door. She is not unpleasant, but neither is she friendly. Unlike the rest of the congregation, my father and mother linger to visit a moment with the pastor. Then we head back home for Sunday dinner.

Although most of the young people from Chama I come in contact with are Hispanos, I know the Smith, Wheeler, and Brasher children from church. Their acknowledgment of my existence is minimal. For my part, I monitor them closely during the spelling bees, declamation contests, and music competitions sponsored by the county school system; register their every gesture, utterance, and item of clothing; study the Chama high school yearbook to learn about the offices they hold and honors they receive; and follow their families' doings and fortunes in the newsletter published by the Northern Rio Arriba Rural Electrification Association.

My mother gets out of the car. I follow her up the walk to the entrance, where she rings the bell. The sunlight at Chama's 8,000-foot elevation is intense and reflects off the manse's whitewashed walls. My mother lowers her head and shades her eyes. The front door opens slightly, and the pastor's wife motions for us to come around to the back. We cut across the lawn and make our way carefully through untended shrubbery still wet with dew. The warm air smells of pine needles and pinesap. As we enter the shade at the back of the manse, the fresh smell of pine is displaced by the acrid odor of moist coal cinders. The backyard is dark and bare. Tall firs cut out the light, making it cold and dank as well. I am glad to be wearing a light jacket. The manse has a screened back porch, and my mother pulls on the handle to the entry door, but it is latched. As the door to the main structure opens, I catch a whiff of butane. The pastor's wife greets us from the doorjamb to the kitchen. "Good morning, Gaby," she calls out with breezy familiarity. "What can I do for you?"

I feel my mother stiffen next to me. She is dressed casually, in jeans and a flannel shirt. Ours is not a social visit. We are running an errand. I become conscious of my wrinkled shirt and zip my jacket slightly. "Not a damned thing," my mother says. I look down in embarrassment. I notice that my boots are scuffed. When I raise my head it is to look away, to a patch of sunlight between the church and the manse. "But if you'd like to do something for yourself," my mother continues, "there's a crate of apples and a box of pears for you in the trunk of my car. You'll also find tomatoes, chile, and melons in the backseat."

My mother turns to leave. I follow, my arms out in front of me to keep the bushes from striking me as they snap back. When we reach the car she opens the trunk and, before I can react, pulls out the box of pears and sets it on the walk. I reach in and pick up the crate of apples. As I turn, I see the pastor's wife running up the front walk. The blood has drained from her face, but her neck is flushed. Their small terrier comes up behind her to yap at us. She is wringing her hands on her apron, but she drops it as I hand her the apples. By the time I turn around, my mother has deposited the basket with the tomatoes and chile at the gate to the yard. I pick up the box of melons and do likewise.

"You have a good day," my mother says as she gets into the driver's seat. I nod my leave and scamper to the passenger side. My mother turns the car around and heads back down the main street. As we drive off, I look back. The pastor's wife stands in front of the manse, the crate of apples in her arms, looking as if she is going to cry. The box of pears is still on the walk, next to the tomatoes, honeydew melons, and chile. The reds and greens and yellows of my grandparents' bounty stand out against the white picket fence. It is only then that I notice my jeans are wet with dew. I feel moisture on my forearm and look down to see some blood from a scratch. I look at my mother from the

corner of my eye. She stares straight ahead, her lips tightly pursed. I know better than to ask if I can take the wheel on the return trip.

Below the main street, on the floodplain, is the defunct railhead with its soot-stained depot, fuel sheds, and shops. Dilapidated railroad cars rust on the sidings. Coal dust and cinders blacken the clay soil of the riverbed. In the ridges above them, partially obscured by clumps of scrub oak, are tree stumps, the remains of what were once huge stands of *pino real*, the regal Douglas fir of the Rocky Mountains.

We drive down the river valley toward home. Scattered along the highway lies the detritus of long-abandoned lumber mills. The surrounding area is cleared of sagebrush and scrub oak, exposing yellowish soil and sandstone to the wind and rain. Small arroyos have already begun to form. From the top of the foothills I can make out the steeple of the Santo Niño Church in Tierra Amarilla. As we drive past the San José Church in Los Ojos, Father Austin is

pulling into the rectory for lunch. I wave to my friend Valentín, who is playing basketball on the playground of the adjacent parochial school. My mother pulls off the road in the plaza in front of the church and motions for me to take the wheel. She gets out, and I slide over. While I wait for her to get in the passenger side I look north and east, to the Brazos Meadows and the Brazos Peaks. It is a view I take in every day, one I never tire of seeing.

On our way out of town I honk at my schoolmates Maria Luisa and Leontina, who are walking back from church. My girlfriend is still not to be seen, but her mother waves as we drive by. Her younger brothers are sitting at the edge of the porch, and the sheepdogs lie next to them. There is no one at the Baptist church or clinic. We drive by the camposanto at the top of the canyon, and my mother finally speaks. "When your father moved here after you were born," she says, "we would drive to Chama for services. We thought for a time that we might transfer our memberships there." I nod but keep my eyes on the road. "I don't know why, but we never did. Your dad is still a member of the church in Old Town Las Vegas, and I remain on the rolls in Las Truchas where I was baptized."

When we get home, I load our camping cookware, produce, and foodstuffs into the car while my mother fixes sandwiches. My father sits at the kitchen table, making leaders to attach to our trout lines. After lunch we head north toward his favorite fishing spots on the upper reaches of the Brazos River. As we drive along the gravel road toward La Ensenada my parents wave to people standing on their front porches and occasionally stop to exchange pleasantries with friends. The hay shelters are stacked high with bales. Stolid draft horses, recently released from their labors, graze on the grass missed by the hay rakes. The quarter horses only nibble, preferring to race each other and to play games of nip and kick.

At the Valdez Mercantile Store we turn upriver on a dirt road past an adobe chapel, dedicated to San Joaquín. Father Austin is standing by his car, adjusting his vestments. My father pulls over. Father Austin walks up to greet us. "Gaby, Arthur," he says as he nods at my siblings and me in the backseat. My parents greet him in return. "I hear the trout are rising to Yellow Coachman lures on the Upper Brazos," he tells my father. "I'll be up later, after I finish hearing confessions."

The dirt road to the river runs along the acequia, which follows the curve of the valley. On a slight rise at the edge of the *chamizal*, I can see the Penitente *morada*, a small chapel with a solitary wooden cross in front of it. Before us rise the Brazos Peaks, whose rock faces tilt back slightly, toward

the southeast, not unlike the tombstones sinking into the earth at the camposanto. When I roll down the window I can hear turtledoves cooing, and in the distance ravens call to each other. The air currents, warmed by the midday sun, bring the smells of sagebrush and pine into the car, where they mingle with those of the produce in the trunk. I remember the question Dora asked me earlier in the week. When I see her on Monday I will tell her I wouldn't mind being buried in the *chamizal*, in view of the Brazos Peaks, at the heart of La Tierra Amarilla.

GABRIELA, GABRIELITA, GABY

† † † My favorite photograph of my mother captures her in festive attire, a tall, handsomely dressed man at her side. The photograph was taken across the street from the Rio Arriba County Courthouse. She holds a parasol in her hands. Her dress has a ruffled hoop skirt that comes down to her ankles. Her companion is dressed in gabardine trousers, a cowboy shirt, and a wide-brimmed hat. The style is turn-of-the-century gentleman ranchero, and hers is straight out of a movie set in the South. I understood that the dress had to do with the festivities that took place annually on the occasion of our town's patron saints, Santiago and Santa Ana, Saint James and Saint Anne. As a child, I believed there was a time when everyone dressed that way during the festivities. Years later, however, I found a second photo of my mother in the same outfit, but the other persons in the frame wore the daily dress of my *paisanos*.

They are standing next to a covered well. Unlike the utilitarian wells that are a feature of the local landscape, this one is painted and has a shingled roof. Neither rope nor pulley is visible, nor is the bucket used to draw water. The ground is grassy and manicured. The well stood in the middle of a large courtyard framed by the buildings of the T. D. Burns compound: the mercantile store, the territorial-style family residence, ranch buildings, and the quarters occupied by the overseer. Except for the pastures located along the Nutritas River, the courtyard was the only grassy area in the vicinity.

I was always curious about the photograph. It bore no date, and I did not yet have a good sense of my parents' chronology. I knew the man. His name was Tommy Burns. He was the son of T. D. Burns Jr., the region's largest landowner. Other than mentioning that she had once accompanied Tommy Burns to a party in Colorado at a place with the exotic-sounding name of Menkhaven, I had no sense of their relationship. But there was that photo of her with a man who was neither her husband nor my father. When was it taken, and what was the relationship between them? She was without question a very attractive woman. Tommy Burns was indubitably the most eligible bachelor around. There must have been an attraction. Why did nothing come of it? Only years later did it occur to me that the issues playing themselves out around me had obtained previously and perhaps more acutely. Her sister Nora, while serving as her deputy in the county assessor's office, had been courted by a member of a prominent family. They had begun to consider marriage when the patriarchs of the two families, one Catholic, the other Protestant, stepped in. There would be no marriage. Nora left shortly thereafter. T. D. Burns and his offspring were Irish and Catholic, and although Tommy was an educated and urbane man, Mom was a *protestante* through and through.

My mother, Gabriela Barela, was born shortly after New Mexico was incorporated into the Union and shortly before the outbreak of World War I. Her birth is recorded as the evening of December 31, 1913. Much more concerned with beginnings than with endings, however, she celebrated her birthday on the first of the year. Mom was the first of seven children born to Trinidad Tafoya and Ramos Barela; six of them survived to adulthood.

I never had occasion to ask my mother about her childhood, but it must have been a privileged one. Her parents were farmers and ranchers, and until their troubles at the end of the 1920s they had considerable property holdings. Following their marriage, they accumulated capital by weaving and selling Rio Grande blankets. During the winter months Grandpa worked in the Colorado mines, and with the income gained from both activities they bought property. They successfully entered the cash economy in the early decades of the century, selling their grain crops and hides to the area mercantilists and in turn purchasing the latest model of farm equipment and Clydesdale horses to draw it. Mom's father apportioned his large flock of sheep to local herders who grazed them on the mountain meadows of the Nuestra Señora del Rosario grant. She was fifteen years old when her parents moved downstream to the Española Valley.

My mother grew up surrounded by family—Barelas, Fernández, Rodríguez, Romeros, Roybales, and Tafoyas. When her parents became members of the Presbyterian mission church in Las Truchas, she was already enrolled in the mission school and shortly thereafter became a member of the church herself. Her father, however, maintained close ties to his Catholic siblings. Mom, despite her affinity with the Tafoyas, the *protestante* heart of the family, and her mother's disapproval of her in-laws, knew them one and all. The eldest of the Barela and Tafoya cousins, she was known to everyone, *protestantes* and *católicos*, as la Gabrielita.

Our trips to Las Truchas were mainly to see the Tafoya family, but visits to Tía Leonardita Barela and Tío Pedro Barela were de rigueur for Mom. Tía Leonardita had good memories of her. "*Fue muy buena la Gabrielita con nosotras*," she tells me as we sit at her kitchen table. "*Y siempre llegaba a vernos*." Fidencia, her oldest, chimes in, saying, "*Cómo queríamos a tu mamá*." Mom employed Fidencia to serve as my nanny in the first months of my existence, providing them with income in the wake of Tío Isidoro's death while Tía Leonardita was trying to cope with Cousin Hope, born prematurely.

Tío Pedro doted on Mom and gave her *regalitos*—a tiny bird he had carved,

a perfect arrowhead he found, chokecherry jam his wife made. Her knowledge of property matters, developed in the course of serving as a public official and a real estate researcher, helped him in his contentious property dealings with neighbors and relations.

In the Hispano patriarchal world, sons, principally the firstborn, occupy the primary rank, enjoy the highest privilege, obtain the greatest familial support, and inherit the lion's share of property. My maternal grandparents' two oldest surviving children were women: my mother and her sister Nora. Whether by design or by default, they received their parents' encouragement and support. Both studied at the Las Truchas mission school and were later sent to Santa Fe to study at the Allison-James School, a boarding school for girls run by the Presbyterian Church. After graduation they attended New Mexico Highlands University during summer sessions in order to become certified as teachers. Mom taught school in San Pedro and Nora in Las Truchas. At the height of the Great Depression, under their father's political tutelage, they both went to work for the Works Progress Administration, conducting workshops to teach people how to can fruit, meat, and vegetables.

Ramos Barela, however, had greater aspirations for his daughters. In return for his support of the Democratic Party candidate for county clerk, in 1937 he had my mother named deputy county clerk. She moved upstream from her family's farm on the banks of the Rio Grande to Tierra Amarilla. By June 1938 she had decided to challenge her boss for the position of county clerk. It is likely that she ran the office anyway; most deputies did so. Except for the superintendent of schools, the chief officers were not persons of much schooling or learning. Their principal occupation seemed to be to greet constituents and engage with visiting politicos, the occasional salesman, and other officials. The deputy carried out the real work. Because the various positions were subject to a two-term limit, the deputies gave stability to the office. Moreover, most office holders were not local residents and tended to leave for home as soon as they could on Friday afternoon, even scheduling visits with their constituents in order to get away earlier in the week. They returned to the office late on Monday morning.

Following her swearing-in ceremony on January 1, 1939, my mother appointed her sister Nora acting county clerk and moved in with my father in Los Lunas, just south of Albuquerque. Three weeks later she gave birth to me at the Presbyterian Hospital in Albuquerque, during Roosevelt's 1939 State of the Union message. Shortly thereafter she returned to Tierra Amarilla to assume her office, and I came along. My father joined us when school was out in June.

Over the three decades she lived in Tierra Amarilla, my mother was elected or appointed chief officer of every county office save those of superintendent, county commissioner, and sheriff, and she worked in all except the sheriff's office. I have no doubt that she could have fulfilled any of those offices. She certainly had the diplomatic skills to contend with fractious school board members, the political savvy to negotiate the allocations of county funds, and the calm and patience to deal with plaintiffs, defendants, and their families. As a child I noticed that the *borrachitos* and other miscreants were very respectful in her presence. She was highly knowledgeable about tax and property matters, and no one was able to put anything over her. And she knew when to bend with the political flow.

Mom once told me she aspired to higher office, that she could have been elected the New Mexico secretary of state, an office occupied by Hispanas for most of the twentieth century. My father, however, was not keen on moving to Santa Fe, and by that time the country was at war. Given his life experience, it is likely that my father, quite apart from his antipathy toward politics, was unwilling to sacrifice the security and social standing his teaching job provided him. My mother's world became my father's, and subsequently mine.

LOS MERCEDARIOS

† † † The high point of summer, in addition to the July fiestas, was the annual session of the North Central District Court, which started in late June and ran through most of July. The district judge arrived at the courthouse at the beginning of the week, escorted by a state policeman and accompanied by his clerks and the bailiff. The week before the session began, the janitor marked off an exclusive parking spot for the judge and his police escort at the courthouse entrance, next to those set aside for the county sheriff and the state trooper assigned to the area. The district attorney, who also had an official police escort, parked in his designated spot next to the judge's. His aides appropriated the parking spaces opposite the courthouse, set aside for court officials during the session.

I followed their arrival in town from my window perch and then peeked out the door of the county clerk's office to watch them walk up the stairs to the courtroom, on the second floor. The sheriff's office was next door to my mother's office. The deputy sheriffs, uncomfortable in new denims and cowboy shirts, their boots freshly polished, rushed about officiously. The jailor, in pressed khaki shirts and pants, ran errands for all concerned. The janitor and an assistant he employed to help him during the court session inspected the brass spittoons and made a show of picking up trash, dusting furniture, wiping down banisters, polishing doorknobs, and sweeping floors.

But it was the tall and wiry state policemen that I kept my eye on from the safety of my mother's office. They wore black knee-high leather boots and heavy belts with holstered pistols, nightsticks, and saps. Their uniforms were also black, with gray trim. They stood at the foot of the stairs to the courtroom, eyeing everyone who entered or moved from one office to the next, nodding when greeted, speaking—laconically—only to each other. This was a county affair. They were there principally in support of the sheriff's office and to protect the district officials. They looked up when approached by court officials and came to attention only when the judge or the district attorney walked down the stairs. They knew my mother and thus knew me, but I maintained a respectful distance, acknowledging them only when they spoke directly to me. When they looked my way, I closed the door and retreated to my window for a time.

Over the next several days more people arrived in town: plaintiffs and defendants, attorneys for the defense, court interpreters, prospective jurors, witnesses, families and friends of the litigants and the accused. Some left town quickly, a case having been dismissed or rescheduled; others settled in for the long haul. The district attorney, a family friend, came over for supper most evenings, and attorneys my mother knew dropped by after dinner to visit, argue, and tell stories. Occasionally a friend or relative who was in attendance joined us. The judge, well known to my mother, came over for dinner after he tired of restaurant food.

At times the courthouse buzzed with excitement; a notorious case was on the docket, a celebrated attorney was arguing a case, or a controversial decision was being handed down. Interested parties and hangers-on huddled outside the courtroom, along the stairs and hallways, and at the courthouse entrance, waiting for juries to be chosen, arguments to be made, judgments to be announced.

The cases that had to do with land claims generated the most excitement: encroachments, trespassing, destruction of property. The *mercedarios*, the land grant heirs, were sometimes the plaintiffs and other times the defendants. Whatever the case, they arrived in caravans. The sheriff came out to greet them; they were his constituents. Some were *ancianos*, elder members of the community who had been pursuing cases since the end of the nineteenth

century; their extended families accompanied them in solidarity. Unlike the court officials and the attorneys, they could not afford to stay in hotels and eat in restaurants. In the late afternoon, when my parents and I took a drive to get away from the dust and bustle of town, I saw their wagons and trucks in the floodplain under the cottonwoods that lined Nutritas Creek, where they had set up camp.

They gathered daily in the coolness of the brick archway that ran the length of the T. D. Burns Jr. Mercantile Store. The younger folks entered the even cooler recesses of the large brick building to make purchases or browse. With rare exceptions, the male *ancianos* declined to do so, remembering that T. D. Burns's father had appropriated much of the Tierra Amarilla Land Grant. They preferred to trade at the Rio Arriba Cash Store, owned by our neighbor Don Victoriano, or to cross the street and shop at F. H. Strauss Mercantile. For the most part, the *mercedarios* stood quietly or talked to each other. Whenever their counsel emerged from the courthouse, they gathered around him and listened as he briefed them. When their case was heard they filed into the courtroom, occupying every seat. During the jury's deliberations they stood in the hallways and along the stairwells, fearful of not hearing that the jury had returned a verdict. If the deliberations were lengthy they wandered out, leaving one of the younger members to keep them posted. When the bailiff emerged from the judge's chamber to announce the jury's return, the atmosphere became charged. The state policemen walked up the stairs and stood by the chambers. The various parties rushed back in and jostled for seats, settling down only when the judge entered the courtroom. After a decision was rendered the *mercedarios* came down the stairs rapidly if it went in their favor, slapping each other on the back and shaking hands. Pouring out of the courthouse, they made their way down the street in high spirits, stopping along the way to share the news with friends and neighbors. Later the men repaired to Lito's Bar or to the Greenleaf Bar to toast their good fortune. The women and children waited patiently by the wagons, cars, and trucks, celebrating with cokes and potato chips.

Seated on my window ledge one floor below, I could tell when a decision was unfavorable by the rumbling of voices and shuffling of feet. As the courtroom doors opened, the rumbling transformed into an angry roar and stomping boots. The courtroom emptied slowly. Small groups formed outside the courtroom and along the stairs to discuss the case. Occasionally an *anciano*, sputtering with rage, had to be led out by family members. The *mercedarios* huddled at the entrance and in the street to vent their anger and plot their next moves. The state police kept their eye on the younger hotheads, and the sheriff moved from group to group seeking to keep the situation under control. The deputies kept a low profile, since the *mercedarios* included friends, in-laws, relatives, even siblings. The gathering slowly dispersed and vehicles made their way out of town in fits and starts, as the occupants stopped along the road to continue a conversation, consult with someone, or vent their rage. Only when the last vehicles departed were the jurors, who had been sequestered and supplied with cokes from Charlie Farrell's gas station, permitted to leave. The deputies headed out in various directions as well to make sure nothing untoward happened. Shortly thereafter the judge and his entourage exited, followed by the district attorney and his party. The courthouse quieted down, except for the clicking and swooshing of the wood brushes as the janitor and his assistant cleaned in preparation for the next scheduled proceeding.

Those memories surfaced many years later, as I listened to a news report on my car radio while heading south on the Cross-Bronx Freeway en route to visit my brother Ibáñez, who was undergoing treatment at the Institute for Rehabilitation Medicine in Manhattan. It was the third day of what turned out to be the seven-day Arab-Israeli War of 1967. Most of the news coverage had to do with that conflict and the war in Vietnam. But sandwiched between the two reports was a bulletin announcing that martial law had been declared in Tee-ehra Ah-ma-rill-uh, county seat of Rye-o Uh-reeba County, following an armed assault on county officials, and that the New Mexico National Guard had been called out to put down a rebellion by land grant activists. In the following days I learned—via radio, the *New York Times*, calls home, and clippings from New Mexico newspapers sent by my parents—of an attempted citizens' arrest of the district attorney by members of the Alianza Federal de Mercedes. The district attorney, Alfonso Sánchez, was delayed in getting to the courthouse and thereby escaped the attempted action. District Judge Anthony Scarborough, my grandmother's fellow parishioner and the only candidate for public office she ever actively supported besides my mother, avoided being taken hostage by locking himself in his chambers. A Hispano state policeman and a deputy sheriff, our longtime neighbor Eulogio Salazar, were seriously wounded by gunfire. The newspaper reports included a photo of the police car riddled with bullet holes. In the background stood the courthouse and the window from which I had watched the world go by some two decades earlier. The window in the adjacent sheriff's office, from which Eulogio leapt to evade the attackers, was open, its panes shattered. The neoclassical courthouse building, which I remembered as gleaming white, was shabby and drab, hardly the scene of great drama.

SEASONS

† † † Spring and fall were my favorite seasons as a child. Given the 7,500-foot elevation of my home community, both seasons were brief but rich in texture and taste, just like the bread my grandmother baked in her outdoor oven. Spring and fall buffered summer's short-lived warmth from winter's lengthy chill.

Spring did not make its appearance until long after its official date. Its arrival was signaled by the roar of the creek, swollen beyond its banks by runoff from melting snow. Spring smelled of eroded soil and decomposing leaves. Along the waterways, willows shed their hard dry coats and took on a soft verdure. Maroon shoots brightened the skeletal cottonwoods lining the river. In the pastures where mares nursed their newborn colts, the snow melted away and exposed patches of grass. At twilight frogs emerged from their nests and croaked deep into the evening. The piercing caws of crows gave way to the fluty whistles of meadowlarks, the reedy songs of blackbirds, the piping calls of killdeer, and the sweet voices of thrushes. Puddles and ruts replaced snowbanks and frozen earth. Along the borders of lanes and on the banks of irrigation ditches appeared dandelions, wild alfalfa, and wild mustard. While a late snowstorm might suggest otherwise, the lengthening days testified to spring's arrival even as it was giving way to summer. In the foothills the sagebrush flashed mustard-yellow tips. At the higher elevations, patches of snow provided a backdrop for the gray-green hues of scrub oak and aspens.

Unlike winter's resistance to spring, summer gave way willingly and almost imperceptibly to fall. Autumn did not wait for the equinox. No sounds—neither rushing streams nor singing birds—announced its coming. The nights, however, grew cooler with each passing day. Weeds matured and shed their seeds. Harvest's hues made their appearance as grain ripened, then corn, then pumpkins. The sunflowers lining roads and fields ceased growing and simply glowed as they followed the sun. On the mountainsides aspen groves took on

a soft yet vibrant yellow hue. The cottonwoods along the riverbanks changed slowly from lemon-lime to citron, and marigolds bloomed along front porches. Then slowly the world turned greenish gray, except for the scrub oak, whose rusty tones persisted until the first harsh rains stripped them of their leaves.

Whereas most of our neighbors' lives were governed by the seasonal requirements of a farming and ranching economy and by the rituals and ceremonies of the Catholic Church, ours was set principally by the calendar of the school year and, when Mom was holding either appointive or elective office, by the biannual electoral cycle. Because we visited my grandparents' farm regularly we were incorporated into the agricultural cycle, but only seasonally and fitfully. We were not part of the religious cycle that informed our neighbors' lives. We did not attend mass weekly, did not have the obligation of confessing our sins to the local priest, were not involved in the rituals of baptism or first communion, did not observe feast days. I did not have to attend catechism classes, do penance for my sins, give up something for Lent, or serve as an altar boy.

Until I was age ten and a fifth-grader, Catholic clergy and nuns were an integral part of the teaching personnel of the Rio Arriba County public schools. My teachers in first, second, and fourth grade were nuns, and irrespective of whether the teacher was a religious or a lay teacher, the school day started with a recitation of the Lord's Prayer and a Hail Mary. On occasion we were marched to the nearby Santo Niño de Atocha Church for confession. The yearly baccalaureate ceremony associated with graduation was celebrated there.

I was under strict orders not to perform the sign of the cross, pray the rosary, or even recite the Catholic version of the Lord's Prayer. When the prayer called for "trespasses" and "trespassers," I inserted "debts" and "debtors." Ever cordial with the parish priest, respectful of the nuns who were my father's teaching colleagues, and deferential toward the Mother Superior who served as principal, my parents, however, made it clear to me that we were Protestants, did not share Catholic beliefs, and did not participate in Catholic practices. For me, to this day, the most emblematic indicators of our differences were that, on those rare occasions when we attended a Catholic religious service, we neither crossed ourselves nor genuflected.

I looked on as my classmates participated in or talked about Catholic rites, more curious than distrustful. What sins did one confess? What was the difference between a venial and a mortal sin? What did the host taste like? I liked the recitation of prayers, was fascinated by the rituals, envied the sense of community engendered by Catholic

ceremonies, and particularly my friend Alfonso's service as an altar boy. Surreptitiously I gave up cokes for Lent, only to succumb at the first opportunity or deny that I was doing so when betrayed by my brother Nene, who monitored all my activities closely.

Our occasional presence at the Presbyterian church in Chama was limited to participating in the worship service. If there was a Sunday school, we did not attend. When I was twelve, however, my parents started attending the Baptist church in Los Ojos, still called by its official post office name, Park View. The church members were the families and employees of Anglo ranch owners and proprietors of small tourist enterprises. Our fellow churchgoers were mostly transplants from Arkansas, Oklahoma, or Texas. They were not particularly welcoming, but they were not unfriendly either. Another group of constituents was made up of military personnel from a nearby Air Force radar base, for it was the height of the Cold War. Many of the servicemen were undoubtedly Baptists, but the presence of two attractive nurse missionaries would certainly have been an additional incentive to attend services. The attendees included some of the officers, with whom my father had professional dealings and a modicum of friendship.

I never asked my parents why they started attending the Baptist church, though it seemed out of character for them. They were Presbyterians. More important, they were professionals, more comfortable with county and state officials, lawyers, and educators than with Anglo ranchers and their hired hands. Our attendance may have been motivated by convenience. Dad's duties as principal of the Tierra Amarilla public schools precluded our frequent trips to Española of previous years, and the proximity of Los Ojos could have been appealing. It also may have been my father's need to shore up relations with that segment of the community, or social circumstances, that encouraged their involvement. Whatever the case, for a time during my early adolescence we regularly attended Sunday morning worship services in the Park View Baptist Church.

As usual, my siblings and I were the only Hispano children in attendance at Sunday school, just as my parents were the only Hispanos in the congregation. I was the oldest member of the class. I didn't mind. It gave me a chance to dress up on a Sunday. Moreover, the teacher was a lovely young woman who worked as a nurse in the church clinic. Although the instruction was principally geared to younger children, I was content to answer when called upon, when none of the other children responded to the teacher's prompts, or when no one else knew the correct answer. I knew the biblical stories well. Over the years I had read and reread the biblical storybook my maternal grandmother had given me as a young child. Whenever we visited my grandparents my siblings and I were sent to Sunday school at their church, and I was thus very familiar with the Bible lessons the teacher was imparting.

On the last Sunday of July, the focus of the class was to prepare us for the summer Bible camp's closing ceremony, to be held that evening. We were to perform. The youngest ones would sing a hymn, while the eight- to ten-year-olds would compete in a quiz based on biblical figures. We would all recite in unison Bible verses we'd committed to memory. The older ones would engage in a competition to see who could locate a verse the fastest. Most children in the class attended school in Tierra Amarilla, but a couple were new to the area, including a boy, younger than me but close to my height and weight. I noticed that he jockeyed for the teacher's attention, interrupting her, answering her questions whether she called on him or not. The teacher was patient. She smiled, listened to him, and then moved on.

On this Sunday morning, after explaining the order of the program, the teacher asked me to lead it. The boy became agitated. "Why him?" he cried out. "He doesn't know how. I should be the one who does it." I started to respond but saw the teacher flush and hold up her hand toward me. She spoke to the boy softly, but her voice had risen in pitch. She then turned to me, a pleading look on her face, and asked if I'd be in charge of the verse competition. I nodded my consent. The boy settled back in his chair, pleased with himself.

That evening we performed for an audience of beaming parents. I presided over the last part of the program, the competition to find a biblical citation. To this day it strikes me as a curious exercise to page madly through the Bible to find a verse of scripture. My sister and brother were part of the group, as was our friend and neighbor Charlie Farrell Jr. The boy raised his hand first every time, and with a few exceptions I let him respond. Afterward we drank punch and ate cookies while the adults made small talk. On our way home my father said, "The young man got all but one of the biblical citations wrong, but you didn't correct him." "Yes, I know," I said, "and so did the teacher." I didn't add that she had come up and thanked me after the program. My father did not pursue the matter.

Many years later I find myself facing the same challenge. The question takes various forms, both friendly and unfriendly. It is posed innocently but quickly becomes sharp. That is, on what basis do *you* hold this position, this title, this responsibility, this honor? What qualifies *you* to be X, get to do Y, have received Z? Why are *you* here, involved in such, responsible for this, in charge of that? Ultimately, it boils down to the question, why you, the interloper, and not me, who really belongs? It is not easily avoided, nor does the questioning ever cease.

I have given much thought to this matter. Early in my professional life, aware of the query's aggressive nature, I donned the armor of my bona fides and laid out my credentials—degrees, honors, titles, appointments, affiliations, and associations. In later years I pointed at my nose and said, Because I have a good nose. And in response to quizzical looks I would add, I can smell money and trouble a long distance away.

These days I do not display my credentials. They provide hardly any protection, and few are impressed by them. Nor do I attempt to be ironic. Irony is wasted in a world where subtlety is no longer valued. Instead I say, Privilege, duty, and serendipity. My answer bemuses or intrigues. Aggressors quickly disengage. They seek a reaction and not a response. The self-satisfied moo and move on to graze elsewhere. Only the foolish, or the innocent, or the truly curious pursue the matter.

DON SANTIAGO Y LAS DOLORES

† † † The bell at the Santo Niño de Atocha Church began tolling in midafternoon, and news of the accident spread rapidly through the community. Don Santiago and his family were returning from a late summer outing in Colorado. The pickup transporting the party had overturned, crushing two of the several children riding in the back and injuring the others. One of the dead girls was two grades ahead of me; the other was my sister's classmate. Their grandfather, Don Santiago, who was driving, suffered serious injuries.

As custom required, my parents called on the family that evening to extend our sympathies. We first paid our respects to the living and injured. The visitation took place in the grandparents' living room, which doubled as a bedroom. Visitors lined the walls, the women sitting, the men standing. A kerosene lamp projected their elongated shadows on the room.

One of the daughters placed a hot-water bottle under her father. He had no visible injuries yet was clearly in pain. Through the door to the kitchen I spotted another daughter helping out, even though her left arm was in a sling. Her face was bruised, and her eyes were swollen.

That same evening my parents took us to the homes of the deceased to pay our respects. The two girl cousins were named Dolores. Sorrow and pain—*dolores*—permeated the households and spilled into the patios. The anguish of the grieving families was patent. The doting parents had lost a child, but they could hardly be angry with a loving grandfather.

Equally anguishing were the girls' burials. The bell tolled as the caskets were rolled out of the Santo Niño church and placed in the hearses. My father and I joined the long line of vehicles to the camposanto, located in the *chamizal* overlooking the Chama River Valley. We parked at a distance from the cemetery. I followed my father to the gravesite. It had not rained, and the ruts that remained from the previous burial were collapsing inward. A fine powder the color of the earth piled up next to the burial site covered our shoes and pant cuffs. As we walked toward the sepulchre I looked at the sites of previous burials. Those of prominent families had granite tombstones bearing the familial patronyms, the plots ringed by wrought-metal or woven-wire fences. Hardy lilac bushes, some grown so large that they obscured the gravestones, were planted inside the enclosures. It was late summer, and in the absence of rain the leaves were dry and brittle, more grayish than green. Simple white marble tablets signaling the grave of a military veteran stood out here and there. More numerous, however, were the gravesites of the less affluent, marked by elaborately wrought but deteriorating flagstone tombstones, wooden crosses, or

concrete gravestones. Sagebrush and prickly pear cacti grew within the confines of the cemetery, protected from harrows and hoes.

Dad and I stood at a respectful distance from the gravesite and listened as Father Austin intoned the final prayers. The morning was warm. Not a single cloud marked the sky. Crows cawed in the distance and cicadas whirred, now loud, now muted, amid monotone prayers and the mourners' sobbing. From the cemetery I surveyed the valley and most of its diminutive communities: Tierra Amarilla, La Ensenada, Los Brazos, Los Ojos. Along the Chama River to the northwest the cottonwoods were still a bright green, but the aspens at the higher elevations in the Brazos Mountains to the north were changing color. Soon the scrub oak at the crest of the mountain to the east would turn, too.

As the casket was lowered, the mother of the older Dolores lunged at the grave. The mourners leaned forward as if in sympathy and issued a collective groan. Only her husband's strong grip kept Leonora from falling in. Her screams and sobbing increased as family members approached the grave to toss fistfuls of dirt on the coffin in a final farewell. Then she collapsed. I turned away as Franque, her husband, put his mouth over her nose and tried to resuscitate her. Dad and I walked back to the car in silence. When I looked back, Franque was carrying Leonora to the funeral car.

Later that afternoon we drove past the camposanto on our way to Dad's favorite fishing spot on the Chama River. The clouds moving eastward across the valley resembled flocks of sheep. The sun's rays cut through the clouds, some of them beaming down on the camposanto. Dora, my classmate, told me on our walks to school that they were the pathways that led the souls of the deceased to heaven. To me they resembled the beams emanating from Christ in the picture that hung in my grandmother's living room, as He manifested himself to his disciples after his resurrection.

Ir al chile. That was the expression my peers used for attendance at wakes during my youth. It stemmed from the meals served on those occasions, which involved all-night vigils and the innumerable out-of-town guests who needed to be fed. Chile was part of my *paisanos*' daily fare and complemented the other offerings: fried meat, potatoes, boiled beans. And chile, made with the powder produced by grinding the ripe pods, was the fastest, simplest dish to make.

Along with baptisms, first communions, and weddings, wakes and funerals were occasions when the residents of the Rio Arriba's ranchitos and plazas came together. But wakes and funerals were not private affairs; they involved not only family and friends but also neighbors, members of the local and surrounding parishes, merchants, public officials, and, most important, *los penitentes*, the local chapter of the Order of St. Francis. While we, not being Catholics, did not attend the rosaries and funeral masses, we were present at the wakes and joined the burial processions to the camposanto.

Wakes were major social events that went on for several days, since family members came from Colorado, Utah, Wyoming, or California to bid farewell to the deceased. Relatives from outlying local areas came for the duration and were housed with family and friends. The visits to view the body and extend condolences to the family typically took place in the evening and brought together people from the adjacent communities.

My childhood memory of wakes, specifically those in summer and fall, was one of great excitement, given the presence of large numbers of children among the families who gathered at the home of the deceased. Some were my schoolmates, but most were strangers. All but the infants and toddlers were consigned to the portales and patios of the houses where the viewing took place. We looked each other over warily, but the bolder ones soon started a game of tag and most joined in. Tag morphed into kick-the-can and we all scrambled to hide. From time to time someone would emerge from the house to quiet us down, but the lulls were temporary. Mom and Dad never stayed long, but they used the opportunity to visit with friends and acquaintances, and my siblings and I joined in the games.

Less happy were memories from my adolescent years. Unlike earlier years, when the deceased was usually an elderly person I sometimes didn't know, in my teenage years I knew the dead, some of which included schoolmates, young adults, relatives, and family friends who had died in accidents or from illness. Especially memorable were those involving multiple deaths as a consequence of automobile accidents.

By age ten I had attended numerous funerals, but until the Martínez family accident I had never witnessed anyone dying. I recall the scene vividly more than a half century later. To this day I wonder why Don Santiago was not at a hospital and whether a doctor had examined him. To be sure, the nearest hospital was many miles away, and it's possible that the local doctor had rendered his judgment at the scene.

Don Santiago died a few days later, and we repeated the process. The ruts on the dirt road had been pulverized by the previous week's traffic. As we walked down the road leading into the camposanto, the mourners held handkerchiefs to their faces to protect themselves from the fine dust that rose up. The evening temperatures had dropped, and the aspens in the mountains had taken on the hue of the sunflowers growing along the highway. The scrub oak at the higher elevations was beginning to turn the color of the rusting metal fencing. The lilac bushes were even scrawnier than before, and the prickly pear had begun to shrivel for lack of moisture. Only the sagebrush remained immutable.

I do not recall any talk of eating chile at the Martínez family wakes or funerals. The tragic nature of the events left even the most blasé of my peers somber and mute.

SHARP-TONGUED

† † † It is always difficult to separate nature from nurture. I cannot say which personality traits I inherited from my parents and which were the function of my social environment. I was nurtured in institutional settings and learned to read social texts long before I was trained to analyze literary ones. My mother occupied political and social space with confidence, knew whom to greet and how to do so. Dad, more highly educated than his peers and an able administrator, was at ease in his educational realm.

Both were tough of mind and savvy about the ways of clients, colleagues, and charges. Dad did not suffer fools and did not back down when confronted, but he did not present any sharp edges. I inherited my mother's quick temper and her equally quick tongue. Like her, I had to learn to keep my temper in check. I have spent my life biting my tongue. As a consequence it is shorter but no less sharp. Unlike her, I did not give my tongue license to lash out at snobbery and insensitivity. I have suffered the insensitivities of paternalistic fools gladly, smiled as they patronized me, and wasted my wit on bigots too ignorant to recognize it.

If anything marked my parents' praxis, it was their values. The offspring of

Presbyterian parents and grandparents, I grew up in a Calvinist environment. Calvinists have historically believed they are chosen people. As a child I didn't understand the advantages of being among the chosen, but I certainly knew the obligations: diligence, honesty, integrity, compassion, discretion, righteousness, duty. At the top of the list was duty, but it was inseparable from the others. I was expected to meet responsibilities both stated and unstated, however grudgingly I might do so. I had an obligation to speak up and to speak out, whatever the consequences. And it was my duty to take on tasks and to carry them out well, no matter how burdensome. Not meeting one's obligations or addressing one's responsibilities was shameful. Or, in the Hispano world, *no tener vergüenza*, to be without shame.

My parents felt it their duty to be good neighbors, citizens, public servants. *Haz bien y no digas a quien*, one of my maternal grandmother's sayings, marked their way of being. They admonished us to do well by others but not to boast about it. Years later, on my visits to some of my parents' longtime friends in the Rio Arriba, they related instances of my parents' actions: driving townspeople to Dr. Becker's office in Chama to lance a festering infection or to the hospital in Española to attend to a limb mangled by farm machinery; extending loans and financial gifts to tide friends over during a prolonged hospital stay or following a house fire; giving refuge to spouses when husbands vented their alcohol-driven rage on them; providing employment for neighbors who had exhausted their credit at local establishments and were skimping on meals while waiting for a remittance from husbands or sons.

And my parents did well by their children. As a child I was envious of friends who had the latest *Batman* comic books or a new cap pistol, the wherewithal to buy a Nehi orange soda and a bag of peanuts at a basketball game, money to spend when a down-at-the-heels troupe set up their sleazy carnival rides in the vacant lot between our home and the courthouse. Rather than material gifts and spending money, we received the gifts of privilege and advantage: books, music, instruments, lessons, performances, summer camp, trips in and out of state, and educational opportunities. When my sister Concha outgrew her beginning piano teacher, Dad drove her to Santa Fe twice a month for lessons, a four-hour round trip, over a period of several years. The summer before my junior year in college, I realized that in order to excel academically, I needed more time to study. A monthly allowance from my parents, representing a tenth of their income, permitted me to quit my part-time job and dedicate myself to my studies for the following two years.

The only other thing required in exchange, beyond excelling in our studies and being dutiful, was that we not put on airs. We were to act with discretion in all matters, particularly in our speech. "Indiscreet" was the first fifty-cent word I learned. Acting with discretion was probably the first rule I flunked. To live in a small town is to live exposed. Life as the principal's and the Protestants' kid took place under a magnifying glass, and what I said and did was monitored and diffused widely.

One commits indiscretions, but one also experiences them, sometimes in the most unexpected ways. Almost three decades after I graduated from high school I was invited to give a keynote address at the annual conference of a California education association. The association president, who turned out to be my former high school teacher, gave me the most indiscreet introduction I have ever had. "I've known our speaker," he said, "for over thirty years, although I've not seen him for at least thirty. My fellow teachers and I knew him and his two buddies as *los cabroncitos.*" I'd been called names all my life, some exceedingly offensive, but I'd never been called a little bastard publicly.

Against my wishes, my parents sent me off to boarding school in my senior year of high school. I did not want to leave my *querencia*. My father had been dismissed as principal of the Tierra Amarilla schools and reassigned as a teacher in the neighboring town of Chama. The excuse my parents offered for their decision was that if the school wasn't good enough for Dad, it wasn't good enough for his children. My siblings were too young for boarding school and thus traveled daily with Dad to Chama. But I was enrolled at the Menaul School of the Presbyterian Church in Albuquerque, my father's alma mater.

Despite my disgruntlement, I agreed with my parents on the matter of Dad's dismissal. Politics, I believed, and not his professional performances were at issue. I also felt some responsibility in the matter, since I had quarreled with the superintendent's nephew and Dad had intervened in the minor set-to. What sealed the matter was my mother's sharp and pointed response to my protestations: "The young women in this town leave only if their husbands take them away, and the young men leave only when they get drafted or volunteer for military service. The men return to their mothers' apron strings as soon as they can. They become shiftless bums. You are not going to be one of them."

It was a telling blow. Being shiftless was one of the two ultimate sins. The other was not doing one's duty. Both were related to having no shame. I knew the people she was referring to. Many were veterans of World War II or the Korean War. The younger winos worked hard at menial jobs and blew their earnings in a binge; the older ones hung around the bars hoping someone would share a bottle with them. Most of the young men who remained in the community escaped the curse of alcoholism but spent their lives making do as clerks, janitors, and ranch hands. I saw them at school events—athletic matches, artistic and cultural performances, graduation ceremonies. Some had seemed heroic in high school, yet I had seen them age and diminish over time.

My unhappiness ended shortly after I was dropped off at the Menaul School on a Sunday afternoon in August, the day before classes began. The housemother provided linens and introduced me to my new roommates. After I unpacked my suitcases and made my bed I followed my roommates to the dining hall. I had been dreading the meal. Dad had told us on multiple occasions how homesick he was during his first year there, and what he missed most was his mother's cooking. The food, however, was familiar and tasty, and there was plenty of bread and butter to compensate for those dishes I was unfamiliar with and thus disdained.

On the way back to the dorm after dinner I asked my roommates what was next. Visiting hours, they informed me, followed by Sunday night assembly. "Visiting hours?" I asked. "Yes," they answered, "at the girls' dorm." Whatever reservations I had about being shipped off to boarding school ended right then. Girls. Lots of them. And no parents. Moreover, for the first time in my life I was among other Protestant youth. Even though a good many of my classmates were Catholic, I was no longer the odd man out.

Many years later, when my father was in his eighties and long widowed, my wife, Antonia, asked him why he and Mom had sent me to boarding school. Ever the historian, she probed into my life experience, so very different from hers. The story I relayed, about the local school not being good enough for Dad's children, did not ring true to her. "We were concerned that he would get some girl in trouble and that the family would see in us a good opportunity to improve their situation," my father said. "It was a very poor community. If that was going to happen, at least we hoped she might be a *protestante*." In retrospect it is clear that my parents saw me becoming part of the Catholic world, and one slip might send me down the slope.

I remain in close touch with my childhood friend Alfonso. He moved downstream as well, soon after I did. Unlike me, he never left the region and has returned regularly to his ancestral home to visit family and to attend baptisms, weddings, wakes, funerals, and reunions. We have traveled together in our advancing years to the plazas of our childhood to attend memorials and anniversaries, and sometimes just to revisit the places and moments of our past. He bemoans the passing of that time, wishes he could re-create that period and that place. To him it is the Garden of Eden he was forced to leave.

I loved my mountain valley community and regret that I could not remain. I envy my friends and colleagues who have been able to stay in their communities of origin, who live near extended family and friends, who move daily through familiar surroundings. I remember that moment and that place fondly, but I do not idealize or romanticize it. Even as a young man I was aware of the tensions and conflicts there. I saw the world change before I left home, and I knew that a rural ranching and farming world was not a space I could occupy for long.

The Menaul School changed the course of my life. It introduced me to a Hispano social and cultural environment different from the one I had grown up in. To be sure, my parents' world included other *protestantes*, but most were family, and I had only intermittent contact with other *protestantes* my age. Most dramatically, the Menaul School provided me a vocational track, one I had not given any thought to before. I never aspired to be an educator like my father, but the idea of being a public official like my mother was attractive. My father's experience with elected officials, however, disabused me of that notion.

Taking classes in religion, coming in contact with other Presbyterian youth, and engaging with Presbyterian clergy and missionaries sparked an interest in religion and theology that my maternal grandmother had inspired in me when she handed me a Bible storybook. I decided over the summer that I was being called to be a minister of the Gospel. What pushed me in that direction was probably more emotion and self-interest than thought and purpose.

The Menaul School provided room and board to a select number of its graduates who enrolled at the nearby University of New Mexico in exchange for serving as dormitory monitors. I prevailed upon the administration of the Menaul School to permit me to live there while I pursued preministerial studies. During my freshman year the local presbytery admitted me to candidacy for the ministry, and this set my personal course for the next several years. At the university I became close friends with two students, Larry and Lee, first cousins to each other, who like me were members of a pioneering Hispano Presbyterian family.

I did not join the Spanish-speaking congregation of the Second Presbyterian Church, but rather the establishment First Presbyterian Church, and I immersed myself in the activities of its university youth group. During the next three years I served as an officer of various Presbyterian university student organizations, attended state and national conferences as a delegate, and conducted services at rural churches that had no minister. Beyond my studies and obligations at the Menaul School, my life was centered on a world informed and dominated by Anglos, specifically my fellow Presbyterians. I interacted with them warmly and considered many of them friends. The relationship was reciprocated in a number of cases, including serving as a member of the groom's party in a wedding that connected two prominent Albuquerque families.

Larry, Lee, and I were the only Hispanos who were part of activities involving Presbyterian university students. Our social relations with our fellow Anglo Presbyterians were limited, however, to the contact we had through church-related activities. All three of us dated Anglo Presbyterian young women at some point, but the rules were clear. Romantic entanglements were taboo. The consequences of what might follow were unacceptable. A young woman I courted was unusually frank in this regard. "I don't want to deal with the problems with discrimination our children would face," she said when she ended our relationship.

Except for when church-related activities took place at a private home, I entered an Anglo home during my undergraduate years only three times: to pick up a young woman for a date, for a study session with a classmate, and to have lunch with a workmate and her family. The social distances and complications went unspoken. Only once did the issue come up. A college friend, while assuring the three of us how much he valued our friendship, said he could not invite us to his home, as he was not ready to discomfit his parents.

My ministerial vocation ended before I graduated from college. The pietism of Calvinism dismayed me; my unsuccessful efforts to proselytize among my fellow students and my charges left me frustrated; and the political maneuvering that informed the church and its ministry disillusioned me. Salvation took the form of an academic career. My lifeboat was fellowship support to pursue graduate study.

In the meantime I had crossed over to an Anglo-dominated world larger than that of the church. I did so with the ease and assurance born out of doing well academically. Despite the sense of otherness that I experienced as a child in the church and that became highly honed when I immersed myself in the church's workings, I believed I could hold my own in larger society. My expectation was that I would not be an interloper in that world. Little did I know. Over the years I have written and lectured about the experience of being a "missing person" in American institutional life, about repeatedly being the first or the "one and only" Latino to occupy such and such a position, sit on X board, be invited to join Y society, receive Z award, and so on. I came to understand that, in fact, I was one in a line of familial interlopers, and more important, that I was one of many interlopers in American institutional life.

POR LA VENTANA

††† The pastor is midway into his sermon, and as usual my grandmother is nodding off. She has been up since 4:30 that morning, and the sanctuary, located on the second floor, tends to get warm during the summer. I, on the other hand, am listening attentively. The homily is about those who have strayed from the path of righteousness. Instead of relying on the traditional pastoral imagery of the Bible, the minister has selected an agricultural motif. He uses irrigation as his central metaphor. Rather than the good shepherd, it is the good steward of the waters who keeps order. The saints are those who keep the faith, who do not stray away. While he developed his metaphor the pastor had Grandma's attention, but once he started to elaborate he lost her.

She will wake up when he calls us to prayer and will join the congregation in the rest of the service.

After the pastor pronounces the benediction, my grandmother remains standing in the pew. She smiles as her fellow parishioners pass by and greet her. Two missionaries affiliated with the McCurdy Mission School in Santa Cruz make their way over to her. "*Buenos días, Hermana Trinidad. Nos da gusto verla.*" They enjoy speaking Spanish with her. Grandma returns their greeting warmly. They ask me where I will be going to seminary. I mumble that I haven't decided. When the congregation has exited, she walks up to the altar to retrieve the vase she brought gladiolas in.

I remain standing at the pew and survey the church. Unlike the First Presbyterian Church of Albuquerque, to which I belong, the sanctuary of the Evangelical United Brethren Church of Española is small and spare. There are four stained glass windows on the north and south sidewalls, one for each of the gospel writers. Two larger windows flank the empty cross that hangs behind the altar. The one on the right shows Christ with children at his feet, and the one on the left portrays Christ as the Good Shepherd. As we walk down the stairs, I look up at the reproduction of the Last Supper on the stairwell. The same scene hangs on the living room wall of my grandparents' home. As usual my eye is drawn to the disciple seated to Christ's right, next to Peter and Mary, who holds a bag in his hand, and whose attention is totally focused on Christ. At the doorway, the minister, who is fairly new, greets my grandmother by name: "Good morning, Mrs. Barela. I'm glad to see you." She smiles shyly and nods.

As we cross the Rio Santa Cruz and turn down the lane toward home, the mayordomo flags us down. "*Busco a Don Ramos*," he explains. He is looking for my grandfather, Ramos Barela, who is away, buying Hatch chile to sell to his customers in the upper Rio Chama Valley. Grandpa's chile crop still has a few weeks' growth to go. "*Tengo agua*," the mayordomo tells us. There is extra water today, and he asks if we would like to tap into it. Grandma accepts the offer. Ours is one of the last farms on the Rio Santa Cruz watershed. Sunday or not, she knows better than to pass up such opportunities. "*Mil gracias*," she calls out as we pull away. We hurry home to change before the water arrives.

I love irrigating—the sound of the rushing water, the sway of the grass along the ditch, the smell of the wet earth. But it is Grandma who is out in the middle of the chile patch. Irrigation, like shepherding, is no task for amateurs. My job is to patrol our feeder ditch to assure that there are no breaks. I also check the gate at the main ditch to make sure no one has diverted the water. Stooping over, Grandma uses her hoe to shore up the channels and prop up the plants. She makes sure the water flows slowly down the rows, soaking the area around the plants. Every so often she retreats to the shade of the *alamos* at the edge of the field. She does not do well in the sun.

To the east, above the sand hills that border the Rio Grande floodplain, I can see the Truchas Peaks, which still have snow in late July. To the west are the

tips of the Santa Clara Peaks. Huge cumulus clouds float over them and east across the valley. I can hear dogs barking in Santa Clara Pueblo, across the Rio Grande from our farm, and from time to time the rustling of the leaves on the two huge cottonwoods that provide welcome shade from the sun.

The chile plants, which had been drooping from prolonged heat and dryness, are straightening up. The pods and leaves bulge with life-giving water. Although several inches long, the peppers are still immature. The water begins to diminish two hours after it arrives, but we have managed to water the entire field. The ends of the rows glitter with the fine sand and mica deposited by the irrigation water. Grandma asks me to divert the remaining water to her flower garden. We feed the animals and then sit down to lunch.

In my grandfather's absence, Grandma intones the prayer. Like Grandpa, she begins by invoking the Lord, *nuestro Dios*, *padre*, *y señor*, and thanking Him for His protection. I listen carefully, intent on mastering the phrasing and the cadences of my grandparents' prayers, so unlike our everyday speech:

Gracias te damos por este día y por todas tus misericordias. Guárdanos a nosotros tus siervos. She asks the Lord to bless our food, begs Him to watch over loved ones, thanks Him for the water that nourishes the plants and refreshes our souls. She asks a special blessing for me, requests that He watch over me and guide me along my way: *Guíalo en su camino*. As always, the petitions are in the name of the Holy Trinity, la Santa Trinidad.

I enjoy days like this one, when my grandfather is away and I have Grandma to myself. When I was younger I followed her around as she shelled corn, dried fruit, weeded her flower garden, watered her seedlings, made bread in her outdoor oven. She listened to my inane jokes, indulged me in my nattering, and answered my questions. Why was some of the corn blue? Why didn't she dry peaches? How could she tell the honeydew from the cantaloupe seedlings? Why did the wild asparagus grow at the base of the fruit trees? How did she know when the bread she baked was done? I especially liked to visit the farm in the spring. Behind the kitchen stove were baby chicks bought at the feed store. Grandma had me gather clover to feed the nursing mother rabbits. Occasionally Grandpa brought home a *penco*, an orphaned lamb that required bottle-feeding. Long before the seeds my grandfather planted even sprouted, the chile and tomato seedlings she so carefully nurtured in her nursery were ready to transplant. But her most loving care went into her garden, where she planted poppies, gladiolas, dahlias, and other flowering plants. Every Sunday morning during growing season she selected the best blooms for altar offerings.

When I was older my questions turned to her family, to life in her mountain village, Las Truchas, to the move to the Rio Grande Valley. My maternal grandmother, Trinidad Tafoya, was the next-to-youngest child born to Juan de Dios Tafoya and Rafaelita López. The Tafoyas and the López were among the families who moved upstream from the Rio Grande in the latter part of the eighteenth century to create buffer communities on the western slopes of the

Sangre de Cristo Mountains. "Juan de Dios Tafoya, my father," she once told me, "owned a Spanish-language Bible, which he read aloud to us. He wanted us to be able to read and write in English as well as Spanish and to know our numbers. And so he sent my brother Celso and me to the Presbyterian mission school, until Mamá Rafaelita prevailed on him to take us out."

She never told me much about her early life. I have only the stories the family tells. My favorite has to do with great-uncle Pedro Romero, who left home at an early age to roam the world, *a correr mundo*, as the *ancianos* say. Tío Pedro returned to his village of El Valle some years later, ready to take up his responsibilities, which included getting married and having a family. When he first saw my grandmother Trinidad or where he met her is lost to us, but not the fact that he was smitten enough to send his parents to Las Truchas to ask for her hand in marriage. Whether his parents didn't know whose hand they were requesting or were dealt a Tafoya-López sleight of hand, Tío Pedro ended up marrying Trinidad's oldest sister, Senovia. Later in life, and probably out of

Tía Senovia's earshot, he was heard to say, "*Fui por Trinidad, y me quedé con Senovia.*" He asked for Trinidad but ended up with Senovia.

My grandfather, Ramos Barela, claims that he married a *rica*. His in-laws, he has told me, owned considerable land and much livestock. Tía Leonardita, Grandpa's sister-in-law, lived next to Juan de Dios and Rafaelita Tafoya. She remembers vast numbers of sheep being herded down from pasture at shearing time. "*No cabían en sus corrales*," she says. The Tafoyas' sheep were so numerous they spilled over to all the surrounding pens.

Grandma is silent on the subject. Never during the years I asked her about herself did she venture a word on the matter. Family lore has it that things changed when her mother, Rafaelita, died and her father, Juan de Dios, remarried. The family did not get along with Pula Mondragón, the new wife. Matters became even more complicated when her father died. According to Mom, the widowed stepmother inherited all the properties and then frittered them away. "*Lo gastó en punche, el Bull Durham*," says Tía Leonardita, who rolls her own cigarettes. She spent it on Bull Durham tobacco. "*A Pula le cuadraba chupar*," she adds with a giggle, suggesting that Pula Mondragón liked other things besides rolling a cigarette and having a good smoke. Grandmother Trinidad and her siblings ended up dispossessed. But from the point of view of a *pobre*, my grandfather Ramos, she was still a *rica*.

My grandmother has never indicated that her previous economic status held much importance for her. What is central to her life is her Christian faith. Like my paternal great-grandfather, Albino Madrid, she became a *protestante* and brought her siblings into the church when she converted. One of her nephews, Tía Senovia's son, is a minister. I recall the joy on her face when I told her that I would be studying for the ministry. Unlike my grandfather Ramos, she avoids favoring any of her children or grandchildren, but I am special to her. From time to time she slips me money she has earned from selling farm produce.

"*Para tus gastos*," she tells me. I use the money to buy religious books: the Revised Standard Version of the Bible, a concordance, a C. S. Lewis novel.

After lunch I help her clear the dishes. I need to tell her that I have changed my mind about theological seminary, that I am thinking about going to graduate school. That it is literature and not theology that engages me, that I am driven by ambiguities and not certainties. But I am loath to do so. I ask her instead to tell me again why she became a *protestante*. She does not speak for a good while. Her normal expression is a scowl, which I have inherited. In her it manifests a singleness of purpose, an unremitting focus on what she is doing. But when we are working at a common task and I am interrogating her, her face softens and she resembles the person in the photograph of her and her brother Celso that hangs in the guest room. In the portrait her upswept hair is dark, her skin smooth, her eyes bright, her expression radiant. Aunt Viola says that Grandpa once boasted to her that he had married the most beautiful woman in Las Truchas. The portrait provides ample evidence of Grandpa's claim.

"I loved to sing," she begins. "At the mission school the missionaries encouraged me. I particularly liked to sing hymns. We lived near the mission, and I could hear the *protestantes* during their evening and Sunday services. I desperately wanted to attend the services." She pauses while she disposes of the dishwater and then says, "But my mother, Mamá Rafaelita, would not allow it. *Ella era muy católica. No confiaba de los protestantes.* She was afraid she would lose me to them." She pauses and looks off into the distance. After a moment she says, "*Cuando se murió Mamá Rafaelita, me hice protestante. Regalé mis santos.*" Grandmother Trinidad became a Protestant after her mother's death and disposed of her Catholic religious iconography.

Grandpa tells a different story. He says they left the Catholic Church because of a falling out with their priest. As my mother remembers it, the break came when her brother George died shortly after being born and Grandpa asked their priest to toll the bell. The priest refused and berated my grandparents for sending their children to the mission school. Uncle Ray gives it a different twist. According to him, the priest demanded $25 to say Mass, an exorbitant sum at the time. In Tía Leonardita's version, it was Grandma's brother Pula Tafoya who had died, and the priest's refusal to say Mass had to do with the fact that Pula had married outside the church. In any case, my grandmother's head and heart were already with the *protestantes*, and the rest of her soon followed.

Later that afternoon, as we weigh out one-pound bags of *atole*, the finely ground blue cornmeal that Grandpa's customers prize for medicinal purposes and special events, I ask my grandmother about the move from Las Truchas to San Pedro. We are sitting in my favorite part of the farm, the shade of the two cottonwoods they planted when they settled at the confluence of the Rio Grande and the Rio Santa Cruz. "We had to leave," she tells me. "The winters became very long and cold. The wheat and oats we planted did not grow. The peas and beans froze before they matured. Then in the winter of 1927 we lost most of our livestock." In moving to the Rio Grande Valley, they left off being ranchers and became farmers.

I can see most of the farm from where I sit. It is not large enough for growing grain and too hot for legumes, but it's ideal for corn, chile, melons, tomatoes, and fruit trees. And there is enough room to keep a few pigs, milk cows, chickens, and rabbits. For a time Grandpa owned sheep, which he parceled out *a partidas*, on a share basis, but he gave that up to concentrate on growing and selling his crops.

"The most painful part was leaving *mi hermana* Eloisa, my brother Celso's wife," Grandmother Trinidad continues. "We loved the mission church, La Iglesia del Buen Pastor, the Church of the Good Shepherd, and our pastor, Reverend Rodríguez. We cried when we parted." I wait for her to go on. The expression on her face is the one I see when the conversation turns to my uncle Ernesto, her brother Celso, and her nephews David and Celsito, all of whom have died in the past few years. The pain of leaving family and church is palpable, even though thirty years have gone by.

She starts taping the bags and has me place them in wooden crates next to the ones containing the plums and peaches we harvested the day before. Early tomorrow morning, before I head to my summer job in Santa Fe, my grandfather and I will load them in the truck, along with onions, carrots, cucumbers, and tomatoes from my grandmother's garden. Then he will head north to sell his produce, as well as the green chile he is bringing up from the lower Rio Grande Valley today.

My grandfather has wandered widely over the course of his life, while my grandmother has rarely left the farm. In my grandfather's absences she has overseen the crops, tended to the farm animals, and ministered to the needs of her family. When her daughter Nora completed nursing school, Grandma took the train to Fresno to attend the graduation ceremonies. When her brother Celso was alive, the two couples would go off to the thermal baths in Colorado for a few days, leaving the farm to whoever was still at home. These days her only excursions are day trips with my grandfather to visit family or to attend religious services in Las Truchas or Chimayó. On those occasions they rush back to tend to the animals.

"On the eve of our move," my grandmother tells me, "I went to Reverend Rodríguez to ask his blessing." I have heard this story before, but it never ceases to move me. I ask her to tell it again and again. Her pastor said he would, on the condition that she promise to continue attending church in her new community. Taken aback by the request, she asked him why he would ask her this, knowing her commitment to the faith. He said that in the valley there were no Hispano Protestant churches, only Anglo ones. "But I read and understand English," she protested, "and I would be able to worship in English as well as in Spanish." "*Hermana Trinidad*," Reverend Rodríguez told her, "*puede ser que no la reciban*." He explained that she might not be welcomed into their fellowship, and thus he wanted her to promise that if she were not allowed to enter through the front door, she would seek to go in through the side door. If she couldn't get in through the side door, she would try the back door. And if she couldn't get in through the back door, she would crawl in through the window. "*Lo único que importa, Hermana Trinidad*," he said, "is that you enter and that you remain there."

When they moved downstream, my grandparents joined the Evangelical United Brethren Church of Española and sent their younger children to its affiliated school, the McCurdy Mission School in Santa Cruz. Though they remained strongly connected to the Hispano Presbyterian community, my grandmother (much more so than my grandfather) made that church hers, and she has remained faithful to it for thirty years. I do not know to what extent she sees herself as an interloper there. I certainly feel that I am—and have for as long as I can remember. She has never mentioned that anyone has been unkind. If she has experienced rejection, she has never acknowledged it. Her fellow parishioners greet her warmly before and following church services. The exchanges are brief, given her halting English and their nonexistent Spanish. She becomes animated only when the female missionaries greet her.

Grandma's relationship, however, is not with the members of the church or with the pastor, as had partly been the case in Las Truchas. It is directly with God, through the intercession of her personal savior, Jesus of Nazareth, whose portrayal as the Good Shepherd, *el Buen Pastor*, hangs prominently in her living room. Her principal source of happiness and joy is her faith, and her greatest pleasure is attending religious services: Bible study hour, *la hora española*—an evening worship service conducted in Spanish—Sunday school, the regular Sunday morning worship service, and above all Easter services, particularly Easter sunrise services. She attends as many as she can and always places money in the offering plate.

Grandma misses Sunday morning worship service only if she is ill or does not have transportation. While my aunts were still at home, they chauffeured her to services, as do I during the summer months and on those weekends during the academic year when I come to visit. While she may prefer a Spanish-language service, she has embraced the one in English. She participates in the liturgical call and response, chants the Lord's Prayer with the rest of the congregation, closely follows the scripture reading of the day, and sings with enthusiasm the introit, the doxology, and the benediction, as well as those hymns she knows. During those moments, Grandmother Trinidad literally glows.

Sitting in the shade and helping her prepare a load of produce for my grandfather, I ask whether she wishes she had done something else in life. In her usual fashion, she does not respond immediately. But her expression is different this time. She goes deep inside herself. I watch her face. Years of working in the sun have wrinkled her skin. The wrinkles are not unlike the bark on the cottonwoods—deep and defined—if of a softer texture. She says quietly, "I loved *las misioneras*. I enjoyed hearing them talk about where they came from, where they studied, where they had been. I wanted to be like them. I would have liked to have been a teacher in some mission field."

She has been both a good pastor and a good steward. While her own schooling was limited to learning to read, write, and do her numbers, she saw to it that her four daughters and two sons were properly educated. Four became professionals: a nurse, two educators, and a public official. Her oldest son, Ernesto, took ill while still a young man. He remained on the farm until he passed away at age twenty-nine. The youngest, Aurora, only a few years my senior, joined the military and left home right after high school.

I hear ravens calling somewhere above me. I lean back and look up. There are two of them, sitting on opposite trees. They caw at each other several times; then one flies off. I follow its laborious flight south over the chile field and the neighboring orchard. The one that stays behind continues to call. The sun, low in the horizon, is beginning to invade the shade.

My grandmother gets up slowly and teeters for a moment until she gains her balance. It is time to feed the animals and make dinner. My grandfather will be arriving soon.

I, too, have trouble straightening after sitting for several hours. A breeze rustles the cottonwoods. I look up through the spaces between patches of leaves. The clouds have disappeared. The sky is the color of the robe that Christ, the Good Shepherd, wears in the picture on the living room wall. I follow my grandmother as she walks up the rise to the farmhouse. After dinner I will drive her to Santa Cruz, to attend *la hora española*. Only then will she call it a day. I know I must tell her of my decision, but I cannot muster the courage. I feel that I am betraying her. Unlike me, she has not strayed from the paths of righteousness.

REGALÉ MIS SANTOS

††† My grandmother Trinidad was not the first *protestante* in her extended family. That distinction belongs to Pedro Romero, who married her sister Senovia. Tío Pedro, he of "*Fui por Trinidad y me quedé con Senovia*" fame, left home when he was but a child to work as a sheepherder. A sheep rancher from Clayton, located over the mountains and out on the plains to the east of El Valle, took him in, made him part of the family, and sent him to school. He came back home at age eighteen, a convert to Methodism, literate in English, and with sufficient capital to open a small grocery store. There was no Methodist church or mission to be found in the Rio Arriba section of New Mexico. The Methodists worked the Hispano population of the Rio Abajo—Albuquerque and south. But by the time Pedro returned, several families in Truchas had organized a Presbyterian congregation. He was baptized a Presbyterian in 1904. The same church records indicate that he and Senovia Tafoya were married in the Presbyterian Church, but no date is given. Their second child, Epifanio, was baptized a *protestante* in 1909 by the ubiquitous Gabino Rendón, who twenty years previously had brought Papá Albino into the faith.

No one in the Tafoya clan followed Tío Pedro into apostasy at that point. Grandma wanted to become a *protestante* but did not out of deference to her mother. Mamá Rafaelita was a López, sister to the famed wood carver José Dolores, patriarch of the *santero* family of Córdova. But Grandma did send my mother and her sister Nora to the mission school. Rafaela López Tafoya died in 1919, and two years later, in 1921, Trinidad Tafoya, her husband Ramos Barela, and her father Juan de Dios Tafoya presented themselves before the Presbyterian congregation and were admitted into the fellowship.

"*Regalé mis santos*," she said. She gave away her *retablos* and her *bultos* and incorporated herself into the small but vital Presbyterian community established in 1903 by Gabino Rendón and Papá Albino's nephew, Manuel Madrid. Two years later she was joined by her sister Juanita and husband, José Albino

Roybal, as well as by her sister Senovia. Brother Celso did not become a member of the congregation until 1929, but by that time Grandma and her beloved sister-in-law, Eloisa Rodríguez Tafoya, were pillars of the church and brought their familial resources in support of its activities. Tía Eloisa had Tío Celso remove the Christ figure from a large crucifix he had for sale in his general store to hang in their sanctuary. La Iglesia del Buen Pastor thus entered the lore of the Presbyterian Church as the Church of the Empty Cross.

What defined the Presbyterianism the missionaries brought to Hispanos was pietism. Sin was any kind of unseemly behavior, but particularly that behavior involving vice or deemed to be sensuous. Drinking, smoking, and gambling were taboo, as was dancing. In principle, not participating in these activities set off the *protestantes* from their Catholic neighbors. It was certainly the rule in my grandmother's home. Dad and Mom smoked, and Dad was very fond of his beers. But he did not drink when visiting the farm, and Mom smoked only in the outhouse. I never thought she fooled Grandma, but dissimulation was the order of the day. She pretended that nothing untoward was going on.

Much more serious, of course, were behaviors with sexual dimensions. Grandpa's brother Epifanio had sinned grievously when he had run off with Lola, Primo Isidoro's wife. A deeper, darker instance was closely held, perhaps not even known by their children. Tía Leonardita's recollections of Pula Mondragón, the woman Juan de Dios Tafoya married following Rafaelita López's death, hinted that she knew. But genealogist Cousin Lorraine ferreted it out. The minutes of the Iglesia del Buen Pastor record a meeting where the church elders heard testimony that two members of the congregation, the widower Juan de Dios and Pula Mondragón, were having an affair. When confronted by the elders, Juan de Dios owned up to it and asked forgiveness; Pula was furious and rejected any authority the church might have over her. Both were suspended for behavior unbecoming members of the church.

No popular magazines were to be found in Grandma's house, despite the presence of two highly acculturated young women, Viola and Aurora, who were mindful of the larger world and immersed themselves in it surreptitiously and when they left the island farm to attend school or run errands. After their parents went to bed they turned on the radio and listened to the music of the day. With their brother Ray as chaperone, they occasionally attended a movie. On trips to town they perused the latest issues of movie and romance magazines at the drugstore newsstand. But except for newspapers and news magazines, the only reading materials that entered the house were religious tracts. Movie stars and musicians engaged in licentious activities—smoking, drinking, dancing, gambling. The women dressed immodestly, and the men behaved inappropriately. Allowing such music or printed materials into the house was akin to welcoming sin as well.

SANTA TRINIDAD

††† Four of my father's six siblings stayed within the bounds of the *protestante* fortress. My mother and her siblings, though, fled the island of Protestants as soon as they could. Only Ernesto, the third in line, lived out his brief life on the farm. Mom was the first to leave, but she remained moored to the farm all of her life, even after she married and had a family. Nora followed soon after, enlisting in the military when she completed her second year as Mom's deputy and later attending nursing school in California and North Carolina.

Marooned by a wayward husband, she returned to the farm briefly on two occasions, once when I was a teenager and Grandpa's only hand. Otherwise she remained offshore.

Ray, too, cast off early. He volunteered for military service at the end of his first year in college. At war's end he married his high school sweetheart and settled in Albuquerque. He came upstream only to visit or help with the harvest. Viola escaped the drudgery of the farm by going off to Highlands University, but during breaks she was one more of Grandpa's unpaid laborers. Marriage was her lifeboat. The couple settled in Utah, and she returned to the farm infrequently. Aurora, the youngest, left earliest and most dramatically. A military recruiter provided her a life raft. She joined WAVES, the women's naval corps, a few months after graduating from high school. She married a Marine soon after, and when they mustered out they settled in Maryland. Economic difficulties forced her back to the farm early in her marriage, but thereafter she stayed away, returning only for Grandma's funeral and one other time. Viola made the long drive down from Utah to see her and reported that Aurora did not engage with the family but simply circumnavigated the farm alone. I, too, rowed away in time, farther away than the places Nora and Aurora came to call home.

Only my grandmother and Ernesto stayed. Ernesto died in 1951. Grandma was still hard at work when she died in 1964. Because I spent a good part of my summers on the farm, I observed her closely over time and under changing circumstances. There were always chores to perform, most of them onerous. Grandpa placed constant demands on her. He spoke, and except for uttering an occasional *Ay! Dios*, she listened. Grandma worked side by side with Ernesto, my aunts, and me, whether it was planting or weeding or harvesting. As we worked she listened to our chatter and bantering. Except for responding with *No sé* or *¿Quién sabe?* to our questions, she was mostly quiet. Sometimes impatient and sharp with my aunts, she was never so with me or Ernesto, who was not a well man. In the quiet of the house as she attended to household chores, I watched her facial expressions. She listened intently to the broadcast evangelist Herbert Armstrong and had her favorite evangelical radio programs. Normally dour, she smiled occasionally when one of us told a story or a joke. Otherwise her face softened only when she was humming or singing hymns to herself.

Her faith sustained her during the early 1950s, when Ernesto and Tío Celso died in untimely fashion. Celso died first, following surgery. Ernesto passed away just eight months later. The losses were wrenching. Tío Celso, two years her junior, had been a loving brother. They had provided support for each other during the difficult years after their mother died and their father remarried. My uncle Ernesto was her companion on the farm. Like her, he suffered from epilepsy, which affected his speech and health. He left school before he graduated and enlisted in the Civilian Conservation Corps, but he was released for medical reasons after a very brief tour.

I was eleven years old at the time and, as a consequence of growing up in a mountain village far from hospitals and mortuaries, had experienced death and dying up close. During the course of those eight months, however, I became intimately acquainted with grief, my grandmother's grief, shared by Tía Eloisa, her sister in faith. The wakes went on for several days, as we waited for relatives to arrive from distant points and, most important, for the arrival from California of *el hermano* Rodríguez, their beloved pastor, to preside over the final worship services and burials. My grandmother's grief was attenuated by her belief that her brother and son were with her Lord as well as by the outpouring of love and support from her community of faith. But her real comfort came, as did her happiness and joy, from participating in the worship services. I saw the pain and stress ease from her face as she bowed her head in prayer, joined in singing the hymns, and followed the scripture readings.

Grandmother Trinidad, born at the end of the nineteenth century, would have been dismayed at the status of her beloved *protestante* community at the end of the twentieth century. Only two of her offspring, only three of her nieces and nephews, only one of her grandnephews remained faithful to the church she helped sustain. Worse yet, only two of her grandchildren are believers and members of a congregation.

As the years have passed, it is my grandmother Trinidad of all my heretic relatives that I most remember and mourn. Calvinists carry their guilt around like a colostomy bag. Guilt, however, does not weigh on me. What I do feel is deep regret. Not that I didn't become a missionary or a minister, but that I didn't return my grandmother's love in equal measure.

I left the church as part of abandoning my candidacy for the ministry fifty years ago and attend services only when I accompany family or on the occasion of funeral services. The one exception occurred when I happened to be in Jerusalem during Holy Week. I deliberately attended worship services at one of the Protestant churches on that Easter morning in memory of my Protestant forebearers, especially my grandmother Trinidad. Had she become a missionary, she would have undoubtedly made a pilgrimage to the Holy Land. Had she been in Jerusalem during Holy Week, she would have been at sunrise services. Had she been in church with me that Easter morning, she would have felt right at home. Had she lived in Jerusalem, she would have made that congregation hers. My grandmother, Santa Trinidad.

CAMPOSANTO

† † † On my way up to the camposanto in Las Truchas I drive by La Puebla. Grandpa owned a patch of land somewhere upriver from the bridge over the Rio Santa Cruz. It had an unobstructed view of the Truchas Peaks, plentiful water, and a grapevine that produced sweet Concord grapes, so much better than the tangy variety that grew in San Pedro. Up against the cottonwoods lining the road to Chimayó I see the remains of Primo Filadelfio's produce stand.

The highway leading up to Las Truchas from Chimayó has been widened. Its shoulders are no longer the sheer drop-offs that so terrified me in my childhood. The road is safer, but *descansos* still mark spots where an accident has taken someone's life.

The firstborn have many advantages but even more responsibilities. Just as my mother was the eldest of her generation, so too am I. My father was not the eldest, but I am the first grandchild in his family and over a decade older than the first of my cousins. In recent years my life has been one of attending wakes and funeral services. "*Cumplir*," we say in Spanish. It is my duty. *Hay que cumplir.* I was brought up to fulfill obligations. My parents were my models. I know no other way. And I have perforce become the elder.

This is the third family funeral I have attended in less than a year. Rolo, Dad's brother, passed in June; Hope, Tía Leonardita's youngest daughter, in October; and now it is Sarita, Tía's oldest granddaughter. Rolo's memorial service at the funeral home in Las Vegas was spare, with only family members in attendance. The Presbyterian minister did not know the family, responded only to a request from Lala to conduct a funeral service. Our Madrid cousins are reticent folks, and no one rose to deliver a eulogy. My sister Concha and I were compelled to share our memories. No burial either. Rolo was cremated. His ashes accompanied us back to Lala's home.

Hope's viewing at the funeral home was well attended. There was no service, only testimony offered by family and friends. The funeral service held the next day in the Peñasco Presbyterian Church, however, was a formal worship service, the eulogy a rambling one punctuated by "you knows" offered by one of Hope's nieces. Afterward the attendees followed the hearse to the Presbyterian cemetery, where the minister offered a prayer before the coffin was lowered into the grave.

The activities surrounding Sarita's viewing have taken me aback. Sarita, like her mother, Fidencia, is Catholic. Yet no deacon is present to lead the faithful in the recitation of the rosary; rather, there is an evangelical worship service. A minister of music, as the printed program labels him, leads us in singing hymns. Even more surprising is that the attendees know the hymns and sing them full-throated and well. I am seated in the front row with family, next to Sarita's mother, Fidencia, and Susie, her aunt. It is all I can do not to turn and gawk. Sarita's younger sisters testify passionately and compellingly. The closing prayer and a call to salvation are delivered by Sarita's oldest son, Louie.

The worship service held at Louie's church the next day, a full-blown "come-to-Jesus" event with a computer slideshow and amplified music, is conducted by its Anglo Baptist minister. The minister of music directs the choir and leads us in singing hymns. Louie testifies, and granddaughter Reyna offers a well-crafted and highly literate eulogy. Sarita, however, will be buried alongside her grandmother Leonardita in the Catholic cemetery.

I keep expecting to overtake the funeral cortege, since I was among the last to leave the Baptist sanctuary in Arroyo Seco after the worship service. The traffic is sparse on this weekday in mid-May. It is unseasonably warm and dry. The peaks are bare of snow, except for small patches on the north-facing sides that the sun touches only briefly as it moves across the bowl of space. Much to my surprise, the funeral procession has not yet arrived. Rather than the shortcut

through La Puebla, it has taken the long way around through Santa Cruz de la Cañada. A crowd of people await its coming on the Catholic side of the divided cemetery. Sarita's plot, like Tía Leonardita's, is right up against the *protestante* cemetery where my Tafoya relatives are interred. It faces east, toward the Truchas Peaks and the rising sun.

Unlike at Tía's burial ceremony just four years earlier, no deacon is present to intone the rosary. No crucifix adorns the coffin. No *penitentes* accompany Sarita's cortege. Instead, the Baptist minister speaks unassumingly and movingly of her loving generosity and offers a prayer. Louie thanks the gathering and once again gives testimony to God's grace and Jesus' sacrifice. Sarita's siblings place a single white rose on her casket, and her grandchildren are given balloons to release as the coffin begins its slow descent into the grave. Once the coffin has touched bottom, Sarita's brothers move in with shovels. When they have leveled the mound of dirt at the graveside, one brother pulls up in a front-loader and completes the task by scooping up earth from the adjoining area. Friends, neighbors, coworkers, and the minister, having paid their respects, move on, leaving only family. The minister of music asks us to gather in a circle and join hands. We stand there quietly as he prays in Spanish.

The view to the west is dioramic. It spans 200 miles, almost the entire Rio Arriba, from Mount San Antonio in southern Colorado to the northwest to the Sandia Mountains to the southeast. The Jémez Mountains rise due west. Below them lie Los Alamos, the canyons that cut into the Pajarito Plateau, and three of the Northern Pueblos—San Juan, Santa Clara, and San Ildefonso—as well as almost all the original Hispano communities of the Rio Arriba. With a powerful telescope I could probably see the juncture of the Rio Santa Cruz and the Rio Grande, where my grandparents' farm was located; and upriver, the Methodist Cemetery in Alcalde where Grandmother Trinidad and Grandfather Ramos are buried alongside Ernesto. Possessed of acute hearing, I might hear the whistle calling Mr. Cook's workers back to work after lunch.

Susie is on my right, and her niece, Isabel, is on my left. I find Isabel charming and amusing. When she heard I was writing a family memoir, she told me she wanted to write her autobiography and already had the title and opening line: "Behind the American Legion." It was, she explained, the place of birth cited in her birth certificate. We stand graveside following the prayer, and Isabel turns and asks me, "Do you know Jesus?"

In a day already full of unexpected occurrences, I am once again taken aback. Gilbert, her father, is Catholic, like all the other Barelas. "Yes," I respond, "I do. I'm a *protestante*."

"Oh," she says. "Oh."

I am not entirely sure she understands. Speaking very softly, Susie says to me in Spanish, "I think we're going to have to convert."

Cousin Louie, not unlike my grandmother Trinidad a century before, is slowly bringing his siblings, their spouses and offspring, and his extended family into his church and in the process reclaiming the camposanto, the consecrated burial ground that once received us all.

Grandmother Trinidad would have taken heart at the flowering of Barela evangelicals. She would have joined them in testifying to the mercy of the Lord and the love of Christ Jesus, would have sung viva voce the hymns of joy and praise. On Saturdays she would have dispatched one of her grandchildren to take produce to the minister and his wife. The flowers from her garden would have graced the altar on Sunday mornings. When the collection plate came by she would have placed in it the white envelope containing her weekly pledge. On a day such as this one, she would have joined the Barela family in mourning the death of her grandniece, but she would also have rejoiced in the rebirth of her beloved community of faith.

CAPTIONS

ii Camposanto de San José, Tierra Amarilla

vi–vii Big Six's (Solomon Luna) compound, Tierra Amarilla

viii Frozen apples on tree, San Pedro

4 Flagstone grave markers, Camposanto de San Augustín

5 Rock wall and gravestones, Camposanto de San Augustín

6 Capilla de San Augustín

11 Los Fuertes from the rim of the canyon; ruins are at upper right center

14 Spanish Presbyterian mission church, Las Vegas

18 Entrance to the lower Rio Chama Valley at Barranca

19 Piedra Lumbre butte

21 Camposanto de Bernal with Starvation Peak in the background

24 Grave marker, Camposanto de San Augustín

25 Camposanto de San Augustín

27 Capilla de San Antonio, Cañoncito

Published by Trinity University Press
San Antonio, Texas 78212

Book and cover design and composition by Kristina Kachele Design, llc
Set in Arnhem Blond with Ivory display and Crucis ornaments
Map by Deborah Reade
Prepress by iocolor, Seattle, Washington
Printed and bound in China by Artron Color Printing Company, Ltc.,
using 15-micron stochastic screening on 157 gsm Oji matte art paper.

Trinity University Press strives to produce its books using methods and materials in an environmentally sensitive manner. We favor working with manufacturers that practice sustainable management of all natural resources, produce paper using recycled stock, and manage forests with the best possible practices for people, biodiversity, and sustainability. The press is a member of the Green Press Initiative, a nonprofit program dedicated to supporting publishers in their efforts to reduce their impacts on endangered forests, climate change, and forest dependent communities.

The paper used in this publication meets the minimum requirements of the American National Standard for Information Sciences—Permanence of Paper for Printed Library Materials, ansi 39.48-1992.

Library of Congress Cataloging-in-Publication Data
Madrid-Barela, Arturo.
In the country of empty crosses : the story of a Hispano family in Catholic New Mexico / Arturo Madrid ; photographs by Miguel Gandert.
p. cm.
ISBN 978-1-59534-131-0 (pbk. : alk. paper)
1. Madrid-Barela, Arturo—Childhood and youth. 2. Madrid-Barela, Arturo—Family.
3. Hispanic Americans—New Mexico—Biography. 4. Protestants—New Mexico—Biography.
5. Hispanic Americans—New Mexico—Religion. 6. Hispanic Americans—New Mexico—Ethnic identity.
7. New Mexico—Race relations—History—20th century. 8. New Mexico—Social conditions—20th century. I. Gandert, Miguel A. II. Title.
F805.S75M34 2012
305.8009789—dc23
2011047449

16 15 14 13 12 5 4 3 2 1

ARTURO MADRID is the Norine R. and T. Frank Murchison Distinguished Professor of the Humanities and director of the Mexico, the Americas, and Spain Program at Trinity University in San Antonio. He has founded, directed, or served on the boards of numerous national organizations, including the Tomás Rivera Center, the Fund for the Improvement of Postsecondary Education, and the National Center for Public Policy and Higher Education. His honors include the Charles Frankel Award from the National Endowment for the Humanities, the John Hope Franklin Award, and honorary degrees from Mount Holyoke College and Pomona College.

One of America's leading documentary photographers, MIGUEL GANDERT has exhibited throughout the world. His series *Nuevo Mexico Profundo: Rituals of an Indo-Hispano Homeland* was the subject of a book and a one-person exhibition for the National Hispanic Culture Center of New Mexico in 2000, and his work was selected for the 1993 Whitney Museum Biennial. He is a Distinguished Professor of Communication and Journalism at the University of New Mexico.